W9-BMX-695
3 4373 00048688 7

Gale Gand's just a bite

ALSO BY THIS AUTHOR

Butter Flour Sugar Eggs

Gale Gand's just a bite

125 LUSCIOUS LITTLE DESSERTS

Gale Gand and Julia Moskin

Photographs by Tim Turner

CLARKSON POTTER/PUBLISHERS
NEW YORK

Published by Clarkson Potter/Publishers, 299 Park Avenue, New York, New York, 10171.
Member of the Crown Publishing Group.

Random House, Inc. New York, Toronto, London, Sydney, Auckland
www.randomhouse.com

Printed in the United States of America

DESIGN BY JANE TREUHAFT

Library of Congress Cataloging-in-Publication Data
Gand, Gale.
[Just a bite]
Gale Gand's just a bite: 125 luscious little desserts / by Gale Gand with Julia Moskin.
p. cm.
Includes index.
1. Desserts. I. Title: Just a bite. II. Moskin, Julia, III. Title.

TX773.G333 2001
641.8'6—dc21 2001021450

ISBN 0-609-60825-8

10 9 8 7 6 5 4 3 2

thanks from gale

This book is dedicated to my lovely son Giorgio Montana Gand Tramonto. I will always remember squeezing fresh oranges with you on Sunday mornings, and how well you cracked the eggs and even leveled off the flour to make "Grandma Myrna pancakes." I hope we always do it again and again and again.

Thanks to my incredible, brilliant, marathon-running father, Bob Gand, who, it looks like, passed the Gand "success gene" on to me. And to my late mother, Myrna, who instilled in me such a gigantic love and lust for cooking and life that even I find it dizzying at times. I still miss making lattice-topped cherry pies with you. . . .

Thanks to Julia Moskin for being the best co-writer, again. Thank you to my dear Jimmy Seidita for his sweet support and for making me my tea. Thanks to Judy Anderson and her children/kitchen helpers Caroline, Jaclyn, and Billy for their deep friendship and for testing all the recipes. To my partners chef Rick Tramonto, Rich Melman, Steve Ottmann, Kevin Brown, and Scott Batton; agent Jane Dystel, publicist Cindy Kurman, editor Roy Finamore, photographer Tim Turner, associate art director Jane Treuhaft, pastry sous-chef Megan Kehoe, the Pastry Team at Tru, Julia Child, Oprah Winfrey, Mark Dissin and all the cats at the Food Network, Emeril Lagasse, Sara Moulton, Bobby Flay, Karen and Jeff Katz, Gary and Joan Gand, Frank Tramonto (Papa), Lana Rae Goldberg, au pair extraordinaire Kiwi Nikki Hamilton, Greta and Robert Pearson, Judy and Jack Shaffer, Muhammad Salahuddin, Marthe Hess, Ina Pinkney, Larry and Julia Binstein, Jim Kafadar (my friend since Miss Sweet's kindergarten class), chef Randy Zeiban, the Bess Family, Barb Pearlman, Bob Payton, Art Shay for taking those early photos in 1963 of me making mud pies for *LIFE Magazine,* and the whole Seidita family for including Gio and me in the making of the Timpano.

thanks from julia

Thanks to my brilliant and cheerful partner Gale Gand, Jane Dystel, Roy Finamore, Martin Patmos, Tim Turner, and Bobby Flay. All my love is for Darren, who appreciates my cheese puffs and makes me so happy.

contents

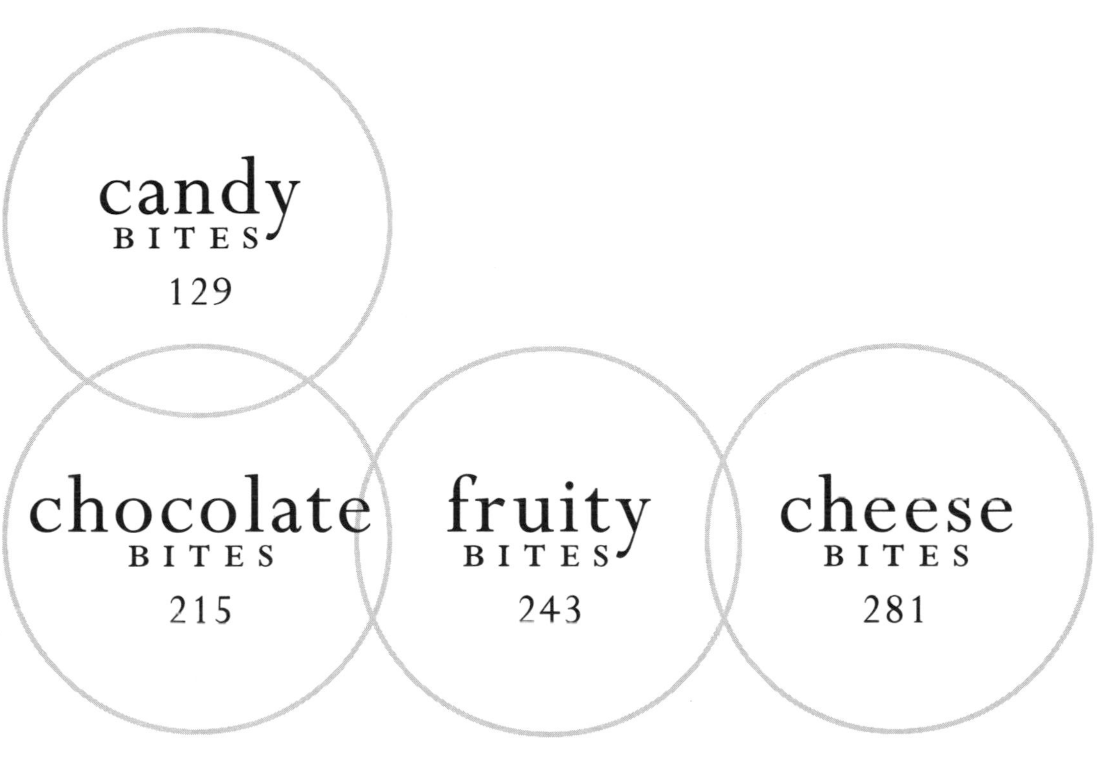

introduction

I know just where it started, this love I have for miniature desserts. It was the batch of lemon butter cookies my grandmother Elsie made for my fourth birthday party, using a thimble from her sewing kit as a cookie cutter. She cut out hundreds of those tiny rounds, sized just for me and my small world. I thought it was a miracle. I saw what must have been the same look on my son Gio's face the first time I made him silver-dollar-size pancakes. And I see that look again whenever I serve an individual chocolate pot pie, or a caramelized lady apple on a stick, or a plate of tiny profiteroles to a guest at one of my restaurants. We love miniature sweets because they are a wonderful combination of dessert and toy.

My mother, Myrna, was a great baker too, and when I was growing up our kitchen was always a place to play as well as to cook. My idea of a fun afternoon was rolling initials out of snakes of pie dough and whirling malteds in the blender. To this day, my favorite miniatures—root beer floats served in tiny cups with straws cut to size, or baby chocolate doughnuts paired with tangy-sweet cranberry jam and a smooth, small vanilla malted—are based on the treats of my childhood.

All the desserts in this book give off a little bit of that playful charm, combining seriously good taste with a sense of fun. After decades working as a chef, I've learned that at the end of a good meal, what most people really want is just a few bites of something sweet—but also something pretty, something entertaining, and something absolutely delicious, no matter how small. For a variety of reasons, many people allow themselves only a little bit of dessert; sometimes they just don't feel hungry for a big bowl of bread pudding after a good meal. So dessert is when I have to get ingenious. In my world, dessert is all about sweetness and light, texture and flavor, and, most of all, fun.

When I'm lucky enough to eat at a fine restaurant, I spend most of the meal looking forward to the tray of tiny sweets—*petit-fours*—that I hope will come at the very end. An after-dessert course of tiny candies and pastries with coffee is a French-restaurant tradition. That tradition was my inspiration when I started creating the *petit-four* trays for my own restaurants—but I was determined to make the flavors my own. It was the most fun I've ever had in the kitchen. I found that my talented assistants also got the giggles at the idea of serving lollipops, chocolate cigarettes, and tiny Rice Krispies Treats in such an elegant setting. At the beginning of every day, someone in the kitchen would say something like, "Let's make a Tootsie Roll, but even better" or "I wonder how small we can make these lemon angel food cakes?"

Using fresh, top-quality ingredients, and adjusting some flavors for adult tastes, we actually managed to improve on some childhood classics and to invent some new versions. I have always liked desserts that make people open up their eyes and say, "I've never had that in a *restaurant* before!" Either that, or, "I haven't had those since I was a child!" So we played with favorite childhood combinations like mint chocolate chip, peanut butter and jelly, peanut butter and chocolate, frozen orange sherbet with vanilla ice cream, and on and on. My Mint–Chocolate-Chip Meringues, Fudge Tartlets with Peanut Butter Ice Cream and Cabernet Caramel, and Parfaits of Tangerine Sorbet with Sour-Cream Ice Cream are the irresistible results.

In addition to the cuteness factor, I love small desserts because I can serve (or eat) as few or as many as I like. Even when I am really full (overeating is a professional hazard for chefs), I always feel unsatisfied without a few sweet tastes at the end of a meal. And you'll never convince me that skipping dessert is necessary. But I do believe that a dessert with enough flavor and fun to it can satisfy in a few bites. And if those bites are all different—say, a miniature tangerine tea cake, followed by a few strawberries crusted with vanilla sugar and then a chaser of intense hot cocoa—so much the better.

I have learned that miniature desserts don't need to be fancy or complicated, and mine aren't. Simply because of their size, they have a charm all their own. I do like to serve three desserts together, and for that reason I've included a suggestion at the end of each recipe for a Tasting Trio: two other recipes that would round out a complete dessert course. But if you want to offer only one dessert, you can simply increase the serving sizes. Believe me, you will hear no complaints!

Miniature desserts are absolutely perfect for dessert parties and buffets. Think of them as the sweet equivalent of cocktail-party finger food. Instead of having to balance plates and forks, liberated guests can pop bites of berry-stuffed shortbread, spoon up coconut rice pudding from individual cups, and crunch on handfuls of sweet-salty-spicy almonds perfumed with orange zest. Many of the recipes are perfect for kids' parties (or parties of grown-ups who enjoy eating like kids sometimes): golden cupcakes carved up and reassembled to look like butterflies, chocolate-dipped marzipan Easter "eggs," and striped frozen juice pops have all been big hits at Gio's parties.

The equipment for my miniatures is very simple. You'll learn to love the mini-muffin tin, which can be used for lots of cakes, cookies, and sweets. When something slightly more unusual (like a pastry bag or candy thermometer) is called for, you'll find it listed in the recipe, next to the ingredients list. I know I don't like to get halfway through a recipe and realize that I have to stop and dig around for the right size baking dish or find the tips for the pastry bag! So everything you need is right up front.

One of the reasons I became a pastry chef is that luckily, I never forgot how exciting desserts are when you are a kid. How delicious that after-school cookie is. How loved you feel when someone bakes you a birthday cake, or how good the first ice cream sandwich of the summer tastes. How mischievous you feel when you sneak a few chocolates out of your parents' private stash, or how thrilling it is when you first spend your very own money at the local bakery or penny-candy counter. Those feelings are always with me as I work; I'd like to bring them back to everyone who eats my desserts. I hope you find them in these pages!

basics and equipment

basics

MELTING CHOCOLATE The good old **double-boiler** method can't be beat. Start with **chopped chocolate** (see below) for even melting. The trick is to adjust the heat so that the water in the bottom is barely simmering, not bubbling or boiling. The simmer should be just visible; French cooks call this stage "smiling." Chocolate melted over barely simmering water will not scorch and will stay melted. If you don't have a double boiler, set a metal or glass bowl in a saucepan of water. The bottom of the bowl should not be touching the water. Stir frequently. Never cover chocolate in a double boiler, even after it is melted. Drops of water might form on the lid, and if they drop into the chocolate, it may seize up and stiffen.

If you prefer the **microwave,** use a plastic bowl at medium heat, and check the chocolate often after the first minute. Stop the process when there are still some lumps of chocolate left, and melt them by stirring them into the melted chocolate.

Melt **white chocolate** in a double boiler over steaming hot tap water; do not let it simmer. White chocolate scorches at a lower temperature than regular chocolate.

CHOPPING CHOCOLATE To chop chocolate, use a large knife and have your chocolate at room temperature. Cold chocolate is too hard to cut, and the knife can slip and cut you. Room-temperature chocolate will chop into pieces, and will not splinter and fly around the kitchen. To chop chocolate in a food processor, chill the chocolate slightly and pulse it just until chopped.

STORING CHOCOLATE Store your chocolate at room temperature, not in the refrigerator. Storing chocolate in the refrigerator encourages it to "bloom"; that is, the cocoa butter starts to separate out and shows up as a fine white cloud on the surface of the chocolate. Bloomed chocolate is perfectly usable and will taste fine, but it won't look as good.

TOASTING NUTS AND COCONUT This is a very important step for releasing and deepening the nuts' flavors. Use this method for whole or chopped nuts, sesame seeds, or for flaked or shredded coconut. Spread the nuts out on a baking sheet and put them in a preheated 350-degree oven (or toaster oven). Check them frequently after the first 5 minutes, and stir every 5 minutes to make sure they brown evenly. When they smell toasty and look slightly browned, after 10 to 20 minutes, remove them immediately and transfer to a cool pan or spread out on a plate, as they cook very quickly and scorch suddenly after this point.

Never toast ground nuts.

Before chopping toasted nuts, let them cool completely. Pulse them in a food processor, pulsing just until coarse crumbs form (it's easy to overprocess and find yourself with nut paste) or chop them coarsely with a large sharp knife.

TOASTING SPICES AND SEEDS This is best done on top of the stove. Heat a small skillet, then pour in the seeds and toss them until fragrant. Immediately remove them from the skillet and let cool before using.

CREAMING BUTTER Remove butter from the refrigerator 30 minutes before trying to cream it. If starting with frozen butter, cut it into pieces and give it at least 45 minutes to warm up. Microwaving butter to warm it quickly doesn't really work; it goes from frozen butter directly to melted butter. What you want is *cool* butter. Butter has been correctly creamed when it is smooth, not when it is clumped up on your mixer beaters. If it clumps, it's still too cold; give it a few more minutes to soften while you do something else. Or, you can just keep mixing it: The warmth and friction created by the mixing will soften the butter quickly. You want a soft, fluffy paste of cool butter, made lighter from the air you've mixed in. This is an integral step in many recipes, so don't skimp on it!

WHIPPING EGG WHITES Separating eggs is easier when they are cold. Refrigerate the yolks after separating, but let the whites warm up slightly before whipping them. They will be stiffer and fluffier, and if you are folding them into temperature-sensitive ingredients like melted chocolate it's best if they are not cold. You must whip them in a completely clean, completely dry bowl, because a speck of yolk, water, or grease can make it impossible to whip whites stiff. Whip egg whites at high speed in a large bowl, to get the most air into them. I often whip them to the soft-peak stage, then add a little sugar for the final minute of whipping. The sugar dissolves and helps the egg whites stiffen without breaking. There is no substitute for **raw egg whites** in baking, and I use them constantly and have never had any problems, either in my home or at my restaurants. But if you are not comfortable using them, by all means avoid recipes that call for them.

We use **raw egg yolks** very rarely, but when we do, we buy fresh cartons from a large market with good turnover (never a farmstand) and keep them cold the whole time we are working with them. We do not serve them to anyone who is pregnant, is ill, or has an impaired immune system.

BUTTERMILK Buttermilk is a wonderful ingredient in baking; the flavor adds both creaminess and tanginess, while the natural acids help keep the flour tender. If you don't happen to have any on hand or don't want to buy a whole quart, you can make a substitute in a snap: Add a teaspoon of any kind of vinegar per cup of milk. Stir and set aside for a few minutes while it develops, then use as directed in the recipe.

You can also use real sour milk as a substitute for buttermilk if you have some around. Shake the carton well, then pour.

MAKING COCONUT GRASS I often serve miniature desserts on a base of flaked sweetened coconut. It keeps them from sliding around on the serving dish and looks beautiful, rather like the "grass" you see in Easter baskets, but prettier and more appetizing. Plain white is fine, but you can also dye it green (or any other color) for fun. Place the coconut in a bowl and put clean rubber gloves or a pair of plastic bags over your hands. Drip in a few drops of food coloring and toss well. Repeat until the coconut reaches the desired color.

equipment

PASTRY BAGS In many cases, the only difference between a smooth, professional-looking dessert and a lumpy, not-quite-what-you-had-in-mind product is a pastry bag. They are so easy to use and make such a difference—I wish I could give one away with each book!

A pastry bag is simply a cone of canvas with an open end for squeezing batters, frostings, and soft doughs (the process is called piping in dessert language). A 14-inch model will be able to handle almost any recipe you will make. Fit one of the removable metal tips into the end, fill the bag, and off you go. I almost always use the plain tips: You don't need any other shape of tips to cook from this book.

Using a pastry bag makes it easier to fill miniature tins, molds, and cups with exactly the right amount of batter. And it's the only way to create the uniform rounds you want when piping cookie doughs and meringues.

To fill a pastry bag, fit in the tip and then pinch the bottom with a clothespin just above the tip to keep the batter from oozing out. Fold the top down all the way around to form a collar, prop the pastry bag up (a large coffee can, tall canister, or vase works well for this), and fill, gently pressing the filling down into the bag to eliminate air pockets. Unfold the collar, twist the top closed, and secure it until you are ready to pipe.

However, you don't need a "real" pastry bag to pipe. Thick, sealable plastic bags make great pastry bags—in fact, they have certain advantages over professional ones. With a Ziploc bag, you fill the bag and seal it shut. When you're ready to pipe, you just snip off a corner and go.

It's best to pipe batters and doughs into the pans as soon as possible after you make them, especially if it's a custard or dough that has been cooked. Once they're in the pans, though, many desserts can be held at room temperature or in the refrigerator until you are ready to bake.

Piping looks slightly intimidating, but it is easy to do. To hold your filled pastry bag, twist the material just above the filling. Hold the twist closed with one hand and put the other hand below it, wrapping your fingers around the filled bag as though you are holding a baseball bat. The bottom hand guides and steadies, as the top hand squeezes the filling down.

As you pipe, you may need to stop occasionally and slide your fingers down the length of the bag to push the filling down. Retwist the top of the bag just above the filling before continuing to pipe.

Most cloth pastry bags are coated with plastic on the inside to make them easier to use and clean. Coated pastry bags can be turned inside out and washed in the dishwasher; so can Ziploc bags.

COOKIE SHEETS The most important issue relating to cookie sheets, of course, is how to get things off of them! I highly recommend using one of the following methods to keep your desserts from sticking to your pans. Losing a bit of cookie to the pan matters more when the cookie is only 1 inch wide. And plain old greasing isn't quite perfect for many miniatures; they are less likely to hold together and more likely to spread on a greasy pan.

I start with heavy cookie sheets, the light silver-gray type. For lining the cookie sheets, I almost always choose no-fuss **parchment paper,** which you can buy at most supermarkets and all baking supply stores. Cookies and meringues slide easily off its surface, and you can lift a whole sheet's worth out of the pan at once, instead of chasing them down one by one with a spatula.

Cut a sheet the same size as your pan, then swipe a little butter around the edges of the pan and make an X of butter across the center. Lay the sheet in the pan and press to adhere to the butter. The butter makes the paper stick to the pan surface, which is especially important when you're piping onto the paper; if left unbuttered, the paper will lift up from the pan as you pipe. **Wax paper** also can be used to line the pans. Place the waxed side down and use the unwaxed side as your baking surface. I also use parchment and wax paper for lining loaf pans and sheet-cake pans.

Even better for many purposes, such as cookies, candies, and cheese puffs, are the new **nonstick baking mats** (rubberized silicone) that some bakeware dealers are importing from Europe; look for names like Silpat and Matfer. They are especially effective when making sweets with a high sugar content, such as tuiles and candies. *Nothing* sticks to them, and you can simply lay them on the cookie sheet. They are easy to wipe clean, and you don't need to wash the pan underneath.

The technology for **nonstick cookie sheets** just keeps getting better, and they are good for almost everything. But this is a case where quality counts: Professional-quality nonstick sheets really work better than lightweight inexpensive versions. Buy the best ones you feel you can afford. Cheaper ones may need a coat of butter over the surface to make them truly nonstick.

CUTTERS A cookie or biscuit cutter must have a sharp edge, but beyond that you can use almost anything to cut out dough. Themed sets of cookie cutters are fun to have around and generally are inexpensive, especially the novelty plastic ones. But I have used everything from a thin-edged glass to the metal top of an olive-oil bottle to a thimble. Clean empty cans offer a variety of sizes.

To keep cookies from sticking in the cutters, dip the cutter's edge in flour every four cookies or so. If the dough is particularly sticky, spray the edge of the cutter with nonstick cooking spray before dipping in flour. If a cookie is stuck in the cutter, simply give the cutter a good sharp shake.

When cutting out chocolate cookies or cakes, use cocoa powder instead of flour for dipping.

When cutting baked goods, a serrated knife with a sharp tip is usually best: It can cut through without tearing. For thin doughs, such as rugelach and cheese crackers, sometimes I prefer a very thin, sharp-bladed pizza wheel or cutter.

A heavy ruler made of metal is the best **straightedge** to use; a flimsy wooden one may not lie flat on top of what you're cutting.

MINI-MUFFIN TINS, MADELEINE MOLDS, AND OTHER TRICKS OF THE TRADE These multi-cup molds—which pastry chefs call *plaques*—are available in a wonderful variety of shapes, sizes, and surfaces. The recipes in this book call for a 1- to 2-ounce capacity per cup—that's 2 to 4 tablespoons.

By far the most useful shape for the purpose of this book is the **mini-muffin tin;** I use them for all kinds of cakes, candies, and tartlets. If you are interested in branching out to other shapes, I would buy plaques of the swirled, round shape called a Bundt muffin tin (there's no hole in the center). I am a fiend for madeleines and so I have plaques for both **regular and mini-madeleine molds.** A **regular muffin tin,** which has about a 3-ounce (3⁄8-cup) capacity, is also useful for baking from this book.

Nonstick surfaces make all of these molds spectacularly easy to use, and some of you may be able to find plaques made from rubbery silicone, which are even easier.

MINIATURE BAKING MOLDS AND COLLARS Completely optional for the purposes of this book—but fun to collect and use—are small metal **baking molds** (also called **tartlet molds**) that come in many shapes, including oval, rectangular, fluted, round, triangular, diamond, and brioche. They come in sizes from tiny 1⁄2-ounce to the more reasonable 2-ounce. You can substitute them in most recipes in which I've called for mini-muffin tins. Always spray them well with nonstick cooking spray; they can be devilishly hard to grease and to clean.

When buying metal baking molds, look for nonstick aluminum and stainless-steel molds that won't rust like the older tin ones (though the tin ones are what you'll often see in antiques stores and flea markets). To keep your tin molds from rusting, after washing them, set them upside down on a sheet pan in a 350-degree oven to dry out for 15 minutes before putting them away.

Collars are the chef's term for the large rings (usually metal or plastic) that have endless uses in the professional kitchen. Collars don't have bottoms, so they can be placed directly on the serving plate, and then filled (that's how chefs make those perfectly round salad servings). You can also fill them on a parchment paper–lined cookie sheet. I use them to make neat rounds of custards and for serving ice creams and mousses. A clean empty tuna can with the top and bottom cut off can serve the same function.

RAMEKINS A ramekin is just a straight-sided ceramic cup with a ribbed or smooth outside surface; it looks like a miniature soufflé dish. The ones you use for these recipes should hold 3 to 4½ ounces of liquid. Ramekins are extremely useful both for baking and for making individual desserts that require refrigeration or freezing, like puddings and custards. However, any dessert that is simply going to be chilled—not baked—can also be made in a decorative demitasse cup, teacup, cordial cup, or anything else that takes your fancy.

PAPER LINERS Paper liners come in a variety of sizes—from extra-large muffin to individual nut—and are excellent for making and serving miniature desserts. The ribbed plain-paper liners can be used for baking and serving, but many of the decorative cups, such as gold and silver paper bonbon cups, are for serving only.

Small paper cups, such as Dixie cups and the paper cones that come with a spring-water cooler, can make fabulous baking molds. Spray them with nonstick cooking spray before baking, then just peel off the paper and throw it away after the desserts have cooled.

SPATULAS **Offset spatulas** come in many sizes and shapes. They all have a blade that's set at an angle to the handle, making them easier to use. The best ones for baking have a long triangular blade with a rounded tip. I use a small one for most icing jobs. The small tool called a sandwich spreader is an excellent substitute.

An **icing spatula** has a long, straight, flexible blade, usually rounded at the tips and perfectly designed for smoothly spreading icings, frostings, and fillings. For miniature desserts, a small one is best; you can buy them inexpensively at baking supply or art supply stores, where they are known as palette knives.

PASTRY BRUSHES Pastry brushes can be flat or round, and can be bought at many supermarkets and all baking supply stores. I don't recommend using hardware-store brushes, even the natural bristle ones, unless you are sure that the bristles haven't been chemically treated. It's good to have a small one and a larger one for desserts, and to keep them separate from brushes you use with savory food. One garlic marinade is all it takes to flavor a pastry brush for a long, long time!

To clean pastry brushes, I rinse them well under the hottest water I can find; use boiling water if your tap water isn't steaming hot. Then I dry them by placing them on top of the oven or dishwasher, or another warm surface.

DOUBLE BOILERS A double boiler is extremely useful for melting chocolate and cooking custards and fillings. But I have to admit that I rarely use mine; instead, I set a metal or glass bowl on top of a saucepan of water. The bowl can then serve as the mixing bowl for the recipe. Both methods work equally well.

ZESTERS I use a lot of lemon and orange zest in my cooking, and the new generation of "microplane" zesters—the ones adapted from woodworking tools—has really changed my life. They are available at cookware stores and from some catalogs. They create a feathery, fine zest with very little mess or effort.

A small flat cheese grater, or a carefully wielded vegetable peeler with sharp blades, will also work well. If using a vegetable peeler, cut only the colored part off the fruit, then mince the pieces into small shreds. Always avoid scraping any of the white pith into your zest.

THERMOMETERS Although it's tempting to try to get by without a **candy thermometer,** you really need one when working with pots of boiling syrup. Sugar burns very quickly when it gets too hot, and there is no way to tell just by looking at it how hot it is. A **deep-frying thermometer** doesn't have the notations of a candy thermometer ("soft-ball stage," "hard-crack stage"), but it works exactly the same way. I always give the temperature in degrees, so you can use either kind of thermometer.

When you fit the thermometer on the pot, make sure it doesn't touch the bottom. You want to gauge the temperature of the syrup, not the pot.

WATER BATHS To make a **hot-water bath,** or *bain-marie,* choose a roasting pan at least 2 inches deep and line it with paper towels or newspapers. This is to create a layer of water *under* the dish as well as around it; direct contact between the metal roasting pan and the baking dish would create a "hot spot" where they meet. Also, the paper will keep the dishes from sliding around. Arrange the dish or dishes in the roasting pan, leaving room between them and making sure they are not touching the sides of the pan. Place the pan in a preheated oven; the temperature is given in the recipe. Then fill the pan with very hot tap water until it comes halfway up the sides of the dishes.

To make an **ice-water bath,** fill a large bowl with ice cubes, then add water just to cover. The mixture should be mostly ice to create the cooling power you want.

Mah-jongg Tiles ◎ Caramel–Orange Rice Crisps

Dried-Plum–Pecan Chews ◎ Florentines

Chocolate Chipless Cookies (with a Side of Chips)

White-Pepper Shortbread Cups ◎ Biscotti Milano

Extra-Spicy Ginger Snappers ◎ Raisin–Anise Biscotti

Marshmallow Moons ◎ Coconut–Pistachio Tuiles

Elsie's Baby Rugelach ◎ Fig Nortons

Thimble Cookies ◎ Animal Crackers

Pecan Shortbread Bites

Blueberry-Stuffed Cinnamon Shortbread Squares

Mint–Chocolate-Chip Meringues

Stained-Glass Cookies ◎ Orange Tuiles

French Macaroons with Coffee Cream

cookie BITES

mah-jongg tiles

MAKES 60

See photograph, page 146

My fantasy of the perfect life includes occasional weekends with no one around but my girlfriends, and nothing to do but play games and bake treats for one another. Friday night would definitely be devoted to playing mah-jongg. Two of my pals have taken up this Asian game in the past few years, rounding up other women whose mothers and aunts used to play.

Part of the appeal of mah-jongg is certainly the beautiful tiles and racks, often made of Bakelite (mah-jongg was big in the 1950s). These cookies, made from my mother's favorite sugar cookie dough and decorated to resemble the tiles, look great arranged on the colorful racks! And if the cookies make you want to play, you can find intact sets at Internet shopping sites or at flea markets. The National Mahjongg League will be happy to send you the simple rules.

you'll need

A straightedge or ruler

Two cookie sheets, well greased or lined with parchment paper or with nonstick baking mats (see page 16); or nonstick cookie sheets

A few mah-jongg tiles, to copy

Tubes of black, red, and green icing with small tips for piping (you can buy these at most supermarkets and all baking supply stores)

8 tablespoons (1 stick) cool unsalted butter, cut into pieces
1 cup granulated sugar
1 egg
¼ cup milk
¼ teaspoon pure vanilla extract
2½ cups all-purpose flour
2 teaspoons baking powder

Cream the butter until smooth and fluffy in a mixer fitted with a paddle attachment. Add the sugar and mix until smooth. Add the egg, milk, and vanilla and mix. Sift 1 cup of the flour with the baking powder, add to the mixer, and combine. Add the remaining 1½ cups of flour and mix just until combined. Form the dough into a disk, wrap it in plastic wrap, and refrigerate at least 2 hours or overnight.

Lightly flour a work surface. Heat the oven to 375 degrees. Roll out the dough to about ¼ inch thick. Using a clean straightedge as a guide, with a sharp knife or pizza cutter cut the dough on a grid into rectangles, about 1 × 1½ inches each. Transfer to the cookie sheets and bake until very light golden brown, 8 to 10 minutes. Let the cookies cool on the pan. Then apply the colored icings.

The three suits are: "craks," Chinese characters drawn in thin red lines; "dots," black circles with red centers; and "bams," short lengths of green bamboo.

tasting trio

Buttermilk–Key Lime Sherbet in Roasted Pineapple Sleeves

Meringue Cigarettes

Mah-jongg Tiles

caramel–orange rice crisps

MAKES ABOUT 16

A delicate, crackly combination of caramel corn and Rice Krispies Treats, with a bit of orange for zip, this nonfat tidbit is wonderfully crunchy, but as light as air and not too sweet. The golden caramel just coats the rice and holds it together.

you'll need

A square or rectangular baking pan, about 8 x 8 inches, thickly buttered

1 cup sugar
3½ cups Rice Krispies cereal
Freshly grated zest of 1 orange

Pour the sugar into the center of a deep saucepan. Carefully pour ⅓ cup water around the walls of the pan, trying not to splash any sugar onto the walls. Do not stir; gently draw your finger twice through the center of the sugar, making a cross, to moisten it. Over high heat, bring to a full boil and cook without stirring until the mixture is a golden caramel, about 15 minutes, swirling the mixture occasionally to even out the color. Turn off the heat and stir in the cereal and the orange zest.

Scrape the mixture into the buttered pan and press lightly to pack down into the pan. Let cool. Using a serrated knife, cut into bars (either cutting in the pan, or turning out the recipe onto a work surface first). Store in an airtight container for up to 1 week.

tasting trio

Peanut–Raisin Chocolate *Rochers*

Brittle-Topped Vanilla–Butterscotch Pudding Parfaits

Caramel–Orange Crisps

dried-plum–pecan chews

MAKES ABOUT 60

When I was growing up, children were supposed to drink oceans of milk every single day for their health. Fortunately, my mother came from a long line of bakers and often devised new desserts that made a tall glass of cold milk taste great. This chewy-sweet fruit and nut bar, which bakes up with a crackly brown-sugar crust, is one of them.

These moist bars last for a long time in the cookie jar. They are packed with "dried plums," as the growers' association now wants us all to refer to prunes!

you'll need

A 9 x 13-inch baking pan, buttered and floured (or use a nonstick pan)

4 eggs
1 pound (2¼ cups packed) light brown sugar
1 cup all-purpose flour
1 teaspoon salt
1 teaspoon pure vanilla extract
½ cup pitted dried plums (formerly known as prunes), quartered
9 ounces (about ¾ cup) pecan halves

Heat the oven to 325 degrees.

Beat the eggs until light and foamy in a mixer fitted with a whisk attachment (or using a hand mixer). Add the sugar and mix. Add the flour, salt, and vanilla and mix until smooth. Stir in the dried plum pieces by hand.

Spread the pecans in a single layer in the prepared pan. Pour the batter over the pecans. Bake until the center feels set and a top crust forms, 35 to 40 minutes. Let cool in the pan to room temperature. Use a serrated knife with a sharp point to cut into 1½-inch squares, cleaning your knife often.

tasting trio

Elsie's Baby Rugelach

Crunchy Chocolate Haystacks

Dried-Plum–Pecan Chews

florentines

MAKES ABOUT 40

Lace-like Florentines may be *the* most elegant cookie there is—but they are truly easy to make. That melting, brittle-crisp caramel effect comes from adding a bit of corn syrup to your cookie dough, which is studded with slivers of almond. A thick, smooth coat of dark chocolate on the back makes them a spectacular after-dinner treat, especially with coffee.

you'll need

Two cookie sheets, well greased or lined with parchment paper or with nonstick baking mats (see page 16); or nonstick cookie sheets

A small icing spatula

½ cup plus 2 tablespoons sugar
9 tablespoons (1 stick plus 1 tablespoon) cool unsalted butter, cut into pieces
¾ cup plus 2 tablespoons all-purpose flour
¼ cup light corn syrup
1 cup sliced almonds, preferably blanched
4 ounces semisweet chocolate

Mix the sugar and butter until smooth in a mixer fitted with a whisk attachment (or using a hand mixer). Add the flour and mix. Add the corn syrup and mix. Working by hand with a rubber spatula, fold in the almonds. Form the dough into a 1½-inch-thick log and wrap in plastic wrap or wax paper. Freeze for at least 1 hour. *(The recipe can be made up to this point and kept frozen for up to 1 month.)*

Heat the oven to 350 degrees.

Remove the dough from the freezer and slice it into very thin rounds, less than ¼ inch thick. Transfer the slices to the cookie sheets and bake until golden brown, 10 to 12 minutes. Let the cookies cool on the pan.

Melt the chocolate (see page 11). Using the icing spatula, spread the flat bottom of each cookie with a thick layer of chocolate, then set aside to cool, chocolate side up. Let the cookies sit at room temperature until the chocolate is firm. Serve chocolate side down. Store in an airtight container for up to 1 week.

tasting trio

Lemon Meringue Beehives

Parfaits of Tangerine Sorbet and Sour-Cream Ice Cream

Florentines

chocolate chipless cookies (with a side of chips)

MAKES
50 TO 60

See photograph, page 146

Yes, everyone loves the chocolate chip cookie. But not everyone can agree on the *best* chocolate chip cookie. With the chipless cookie, you get to savor that delectable, buttery brown sugar dough and choose your chips as you go. I like to serve bite-size chipless cookies with a few Hershey's Kisses; it's fun to get a pile of tiny cookies and huge chips.

You can buy milk chocolate or semisweet chocolate chips—or white chocolate, or even butterscotch chips. You can chop up the finest Valrhona or a crunchy Toblerone and present them in fancy bonbon cups. Or you can try all of the above. The cookie remains simply, utterly perfect.

Make the dough balls in advance and freeze, so you can bake them right before serving.

you'll need

Two cookie sheets, well greased or lined with parchment paper or with nonstick baking mats (see page 16); or nonstick cookie sheets

8 ounces (2 sticks) cool unsalted butter, cut into pieces
½ cup granulated sugar
1 cup (packed) light brown sugar
1 teaspoon pure vanilla extract
2 eggs
1 teaspoon baking soda
1 tablespoon milk, warmed (this is to activate the baking soda)
2¼ cups all-purpose flour
1 teaspoon salt
1 cup chocolate chips, or a combination of white chocolate, milk chocolate, and semisweet chips

Cream the butter in a mixer fitted with a paddle attachment (or using a hand mixer) until soft and fluffy. Add both sugars and mix. Add the vanilla extract and 1 egg and mix. Add the remaining egg and mix.

In a small bowl, mix the baking soda with the warm milk. Add to the butter–sugar mixture and mix. Add the flour and salt and mix.

Heat the oven to 375 degrees.

Using your hands, roll the dough into uniform balls about the size of an acorn or a large marble. Arrange on the cookie sheets, leaving 1 inch of space between the cookies. *(You can also put the balls of dough on a tray, freeze until hard, then transfer to a heavy-duty plastic bag and keep frozen for up to 1 month. Let the balls thaw for 15 minutes at room temperature before baking.)*

Bake until light brown, 8 to 10 minutes.

Let the cookies cool for 2 minutes on the pan and serve warm, with chips on the side.

tasting trio

Cinnamon–Basmati Rice Pudding

Mini Root Beer Floats

Chocolate Chipless Cookies

white-pepper shortbread cups

MAKES 30 TO 60 (DEPENDING ON YOUR TIN SIZE)

See photograph, page 146

Homemade shortbread always tastes wonderful, but getting it perfectly smooth and golden brown can test the patience of a saint—and of a pastry chef. So I was delighted when my pastry sous chef, Megan Kehoe, treated me to a round, warm shortbread nugget—as buttery and melting as shortbread, but pleasantly cakey. Rolling the cold dough into balls, then resting them in tiny baking cups (such as mini-muffin tins) produces a thicker cookie, one that you can gently hollow out and even stuff. The cookies will expand to fit the bottom of the cup, so use the smallest ones you have.

My favorite shortbread is lightly flavored with almond and not very sweet, and I like it scented with a little white pepper. Adding a juicy berry sweetened with maple gives the cookie the effect of an itty-bitty pie, with a quarter of the work.

¼ cup plus 1 tablespoon confectioners' sugar
½ cup all-purpose flour
3 tablespoons cornstarch
2 tablespoons almond flour (available at gourmet and health-food stores), or storebought ground almonds (see Sources page 300)
7 tablespoons cool unsalted butter, cut into pieces
Scant ¼ teaspoon pure almond extract
¾ teaspoon ground white pepper
½ cup maple syrup
About 60 blueberries

you'll need

2 mini-muffin tins (preferably nonstick) or other small, deep baking cups, sprayed with nonstick cooking spray

Combine the ¼ cup of sugar with the flour, cornstarch, almond flour, butter, almond extract, and white pepper in a mixer fitted with a paddle attachment. Mix until the dough comes together.

On a lightly floured surface, roll the dough into a 1-inch-thick log. Cut off a 1-inch length and roll it into a ball, then test the size by resting it in a baking cup. The ball shouldn't touch the sides of the cup, but should be big enough to almost fill the cup when baked (they will spread out and puff up during the baking). If the balls are too small, they will spread flat over the bottom of the mold, making cookies instead of cups. Cut the remaining dough into lengths that will make balls of the right size, then roll into balls. *(The recipe can be made up to this point and refrigerated overnight, or frozen for up to 1 month.)*

Heat the oven to 375 degrees. Place the balls in the baking cups. Bake until golden but not brown, about 15 minutes. Remove from the oven. While the shortbreads are still hot, make a depression in the center of each by pressing the tip of a wooden spoon handle or a ¼-teaspoon measure down into the top of the shortbread. Let the shortbreads cool in the cups, then carefully remove.

Bring the maple syrup to a boil in a small saucepan. Turn off the heat and add the blueberries, stirring gently to cook them ever so slightly. Do not break the berries. Spoon a berry into the center of each shortbread cup. Sprinkle with the remaining tablespoon of confectioners' sugar. Serve the cookies the same day they are filled.

tasting trio

Sesame Brittle

Fairground Apple Fritters

White-Pepper Shortbread Cups

biscotti milano

MAKES 80

Contrary to popular belief, the marvelous Milano cookie was not invented by Pepperidge Farm. It is actually a classic Italian *biscotto Milano,* found in many of the oldest bakeries in Milan. The key ingredient is the creamy sugar glaze (traditionally flavored with orange, not mint) that sandwiches the cookie together. Crisp, flat butter cookies, dark chocolate, and a soft mint center . . . homemade Milanos are just wonderful, and these are small enough to pop in your mouth whole.

you'll need

- A pastry bag fitted with a small (¼-inch) plain tip (see page 15)
- Two cookie sheets, well greased or lined with parchment paper or with nonstick baking mats (see page 16); or nonstick cookie sheets
- A small offset spatula or sandwich spreader

FOR THE COOKIE DOUGH

6 tablespoons cool unsalted butter, cut into pieces
1¼ cups confectioners' sugar
Scant ½ cup egg whites (from about 4 eggs)
1 teaspoon pure vanilla extract
1 teaspoon pure lemon extract
¾ cup all-purpose flour

FOR THE MINT GLAZE

1 egg white
About 2 cups confectioners' sugar
A few drops of mint extract

FOR THE CHOCOLATE GLAZE

4 ounces semisweet chocolate

Heat the oven to 350 degrees.

Make the cookie dough: Cream the butter until smooth in a mixer fitted with a paddle attachment. Mix in the sugar. A little at a time, mix in the egg whites, then add the vanilla and lemon extracts. Add the flour and mix just until incorporated. Transfer the dough to the pastry bag.

Pipe 1-inch-long sections of dough onto the sheet pans, spacing them 2 inches apart (they will spread sideways). Bake until golden on top and brown around the edges, about 10 minutes. Let the cookies cool on the pan.

Make the mint glaze: Whisk the egg white with 1½ cups of the confectioners' sugar until smooth. Whisk in more sugar a little at a time, just until you have a thick, smooth glaze. Add mint extract to taste.

Make the chocolate glaze: Melt the chocolate (see page 11). Spread the flat sides of half of the cookies with chocolate. Spread the flat sides of the remaining cookies with mint glaze. Sandwich together and set on a clean sheet pan. Let the cookies sit at room temperature until firm, at least 1 hour.

tasting trio

Double-Vanilla Crème Brûlées

Ruby Raspberry Jellies

Biscotti Milano

extra-spicy ginger snappers

MAKES ABOUT 60

There are two schools of thought about ginger snaps: Some prefer the supercrisp wafer, others the gingerbread-like, chewy cookie. I am something of a ginger fiend, so I like both kinds—but a moist, crumbly cookie has deeper ginger flavor and thus a slight edge.

The taste of the cookies isn't chile-hot, even though the recipe includes cayenne and lots of warming spices. The cayenne is there to intensify the ginger flavor, and then the heat is balanced out by the sugar (a glass of ice-cold milk is great, too). The real depth of flavor in a gingersnap comes from molasses, which adds its dark-roasted taste to the mix.

you'll need

Two cookie sheets, well greased or lined with parchment paper or with nonstick baking mats (see page 16); or nonstick cookie sheets

2½ cups all-purpose flour
1½ teaspoons baking soda
¾ teaspoon cinnamon
1 teaspoon ground ginger, or more to taste
⅜ teaspoon ground cloves
⅜ teaspoon salt
⅜ teaspoon cayenne pepper
8 tablespoons (1 stick) cool unsalted butter, cut into pieces
½ cup granulated sugar, plus extra for rolling
1 cup (packed) light brown sugar
⅓ cup molasses (not blackstrap)
¼ cup egg whites (from about 2 eggs)

Combine the flour, baking soda, cinnamon, ginger, cloves, salt, and cayenne pepper in a mixing bowl and set aside.

Cream the butter until smooth and fluffy in a mixer fitted with a paddle attachment (or using a hand mixer). Add the sugars and mix. Add the molasses and mix. Add the egg whites in 2 batches, mixing to combine after each addition. Add the dry ingredients in three batches, mixing to combine after each addition.

Heat the oven to 350 degrees. Spread a few tablespoons of granulated sugar on a small plate.

Roll the dough into ¾-inch balls, then roll each ball in the sugar until lightly coated. Transfer to the cookie sheets, leaving 1 inch of space between the cookies. Bake until browned, 8 to 10 minutes. Let the cookies cool on wire racks and store in an airtight container.

tasting trio

Brittle-Topped Vanilla–Butterscotch Pudding Parfaits

Tangerine Marmalade Babycakes

Extra-Spicy Ginger Snappers

raisin–anise biscotti

MAKES ABOUT 50

Raisins, almonds, and aniseed—all in one cookie? You bet. Each bite of these easy, texture-rich *biscotti* is chewy, fruity, crunchy, nutty, and packed with flavor.

In Tuscany, sweet, raisiny *vin santo,* an aged dessert wine, is always poured for dipping with biscotti. So putting raisins *into* the cookie was an easy call. Anisette is another fragrant Italian dessert liqueur, so adding aniseed to the biscotti simply rounded out the Italian flavors. Aniseed and fennel seed are members of the same licorice-flavored family; either will work here.

you'll need

A large cookie sheet, well greased or lined with parchment paper or with nonstick baking mats (see page 16); or a nonstick cookie sheet

2¼ cups sifted all-purpose flour
½ teaspoon baking powder
½ teaspoon baking soda
⅛ teaspoon salt
⅔ cup sugar
¾ cup coarsely chopped almonds, toasted (see page 12)
½ cup raisins
1 teaspoon aniseed or fennel seed, toasted (see page 12)
3 eggs
1 teaspoon pure vanilla extract

Heat the oven to 375 degrees.

Sift together the flour, baking powder, baking soda, salt, and sugar and transfer to the bowl of a mixer fitted with a paddle attachment. Mix in the almonds, raisins, and aniseed.

Whisk together the eggs and vanilla extract in a small bowl. Add to the dry ingredients and mix. The dough may seem dry, but it will moisten as you mix. Turn the dough out onto a lightly floured work surface and divide into

2 equal pieces. Wet your hands and use them to roll each piece of dough into a flattened log about 12 inches long, 1½ inches wide, and 1 inch high.

Transfer the logs to the cookie sheet, leaving at least 3 inches between the logs (they will spread during baking). Bake until golden brown, 25 to 30 minutes, rotating the pan after 15 minutes to ensure even baking.

Let the cookies cool for 15 minutes. Reduce the oven temperature to 300 degrees. Carefully transfer the logs to a cutting board. Wipe off the sheet pan and grease it again.

Using a serrated knife, cut the logs on the diagonal into ¼-inch-thick slices. Lay the slices cut side up on the sheet pan, discarding (or eating) the ends. Bake until dry and toasted, 15 to 20 minutes. Let the cookies cool and store them in an airtight container.

tasting trio

Green Grapes Glacé

Blue Cheese Fritters with Pear Salad

Raisin–Anise Biscotti

marshmallow moons

MAKES 65

See photograph, page 146

Homemade marshmallow is one of my favorite things to make. People are amazed when you whip it up from egg whites, corn syrup, and gelatin—those pillowy, snow-white puffs seem so impossibly perfect. The flavor is bright and fresh and the texture lush, ideal for these dark chocolate–coated mouthfuls of crisp cookie and marshmallow. Smaller than Moon Pies or Mallomars, they make a cute, pop-able bite that is especially appealing to kids.

Leftover marshmallow can be molded or piped into any shape you like (including little chicks) and decorated with colored sugar, or piped into tiny kisses for hot cocoa. If making marshmallow isn't in your plans, you can use supermarket marshmallows. Cut them in half horizontally, place them on the baked cookie bases, and warm them in a 300-degree oven until puffed and sticky, about 5 minutes.

you'll need

A cookie cutter, 1 to 1½ inches in diameter

Two cookie sheets, well greased or lined with parchment paper or with nonstick baking mats (see page 16); or nonstick cookie sheets

A candy thermometer

A pastry bag, optional (see page 15), fitted with a large plain tip

FOR THE COOKIE DOUGH

3 cups all-purpose flour
½ cup sugar
½ teaspoon salt
¾ teaspoon baking powder
⅜ teaspoon baking soda
½ teaspoon cinnamon
12 tablespoons (1½ sticks) cool unsalted butter, cut into pieces
3 eggs, whisked together

FOR THE HOMEMADE MARSHMALLOWS

¼ cup light corn syrup
¾ cup sugar
2 egg whites
1 tablespoon confectioners' gelatin

2 tablespoons cold water
¼ teaspoon pure vanilla extract

FOR THE CHOCOLATE GLAZE

12 ounces semisweet chocolate
2 ounces cocoa butter (available at baking-supply stores), or ¼ cup vegetable oil

Make the cookies: Blend the dry ingredients in a mixer fitted with a paddle attachment.

Add the butter and mix at low speed until sandy. Add the eggs and mix to combine. Form the dough into a disk, wrap it in plastic wrap, and refrigerate for at least 1 hour. (*The recipe can be made up this point and refrigerated for up to 3 days.*)

Heat the oven to 375 degrees.

On a lightly floured surface, roll out the dough ⅛ inch thick. Use the cookie cutter to cut out small rounds of dough. Transfer to the prepared pans. Reroll the scraps and cut out more cookies, then discard the scraps (they will become tough if you keep rerolling them).

Bake the cookies until light golden brown, about 10 minutes. Let them cool to room temperature on a wire rack.

Make the marshmallows: Combine ¼ cup water, the corn syrup, and the sugar in a saucepan fitted with a candy thermometer. Bring to a boil and boil to "soft-ball" stage, or about 235 degrees.

Meanwhile, whip the egg whites until soft peaks form. In a small bowl, sprinkle the gelatin over the 2 tablespoons cold water and let dissolve. When the syrup reaches 235 degrees, remove it from the heat, add the gelatin, and

recipe continues on next page

mix. Pour the syrup into the whipping egg whites. Add the vanilla and continue whipping until stiff. Transfer to the pastry bag. Pipe a "kiss" of marshmallow to cover each cookie. Let the cookies sit at room temperature for 2 hours to cool and stiffen.

Make the chocolate glaze: Melt the glaze ingredients together in the top of a double boiler or a bowl set over barely simmering water, stirring occasionally. Line a cookie sheet with parchment paper or a nonstick baking mat. One at a time, gently drop the marshmallow-topped cookies into the hot chocolate. Lift out with a fork and let the excess chocolate drip back into the bowl. Place the glazed cookies on the cookie sheet and let them sit at room temperature until the coating is firm, 1 to 2 hours.

tasting trio

Clementines in Mint Syrup

Chewy Butter Caramels

Marshmallow Moons

coconut pistachio tuiles

MAKES ABOUT 36

Baking doesn't get much better than a four-ingredient recipe, especially when it rewards you with this much texture and flavor. Flaked sweetened coconut is one of the easiest and most fun ingredients in the pastry kitchen; I love that snow-white color, that fluffy texture, and that tropical-fantasy flavor. Lightly bound with egg whites and enlivened with crunchy pistachios, this dough bakes into crisp, light rounds with plenty of body and subtle nut flavors.

These cookies are too delicate to work on plain nonstick pans.

you'll need

Two cookie sheets, lined with parchment paper or with nonstick baking mats (see page 16)

Heaping ¾ cup sugar
Scant ½ cup egg whites (from about 3 eggs)
¾ pound (scant 2½ cups) sweetened flaked coconut
¼ cup chopped green (unsalted) pistachio nuts

Heat the oven to 350 degrees.

Mix all the ingredients together in a bowl. *(The recipe can be made up to this point and kept refrigerated for up to 3 days.)*

Drop the mixture onto the cookie sheets by teaspoonfuls, leaving 2 inches between the cookies. Dip a fork into lukewarm water and use the back of the tines to flatten the cookies into rounds about 2 inches across.

Bake until dark golden, about 12 minutes. Let the tuiles cool completely on the pans. Remove carefully with a thin metal spatula.

tasting trio

Bread Puddings with Orange Marmalade

Crunchy Chocolate Haystacks

Coconut Pistachio Tuiles

elsie's baby rugelach

MAKES
48

My grandma Elsie had lots of sisters, and they were all great bakers. Their Budapest-born mother taught them the Hungarian classics: strudel, poppy-seed cake, and rugelach, which she called *kipfel.* She considered herself lucky to have a large brood of girls to help with all the hard work of baking!

This wonderful dough is yeasty but not bready, and not too sweet. The layers of buttery pastry enclose a sweet, satisfying filling of raisins, pecans, and cinnamon sugar. It's good to have some extra hands when rolling the rugelach; it's a fun project for a Saturday afternoon, and everyone ends up with bite-size pastries to take home. They freeze beautifully.

you'll need

Two cookie sheets, well greased or lined with parchment paper or with nonstick baking mats (see page 16); or nonstick cookie sheets

FOR THE DOUGH

8 ounces (2 sticks) cool unsalted butter, cut into pieces
4 cups all-purpose flour
1 teaspoon salt
¼ cup sugar
1 cup heavy cream
1 (6/10-ounce) cake of fresh yeast or 1 (¼-ounce) envelope of dry yeast
3 egg yolks

FOR THE FILLING

8 tablespoons (1 stick) unsalted butter, melted
1 cup sugar
2 teaspoons cinnamon
½ cup chopped pecans
¼ cup golden raisins

Make the dough: Combine the butter, flour, salt, and sugar in a large bowl or the bowl of a mixer fitted with a paddle attachment. Using your fingers, rub the butter into the dry ingredients to make a crumbly, sandy mixture.

Put the cream in a separate bowl and crumble the yeast into it (if you're using dry yeast, stir to dissolve it). Stir in the yolks. Add the wet ingredients to the dry ingredients, mixing to make a dough (you'll probably want to use your hands or the paddle attachment). The dough may feel somewhat sticky. Wrap the dough in plastic or wax paper and chill it for at least 3 to 4 hours, or as long as overnight.

Make the filling: Combine the melted butter, sugar, and cinnamon.

Flour a work surface and cut the dough into quarters. Roll out one quarter of the dough as thin as possible into a circle. Spread or brush one quarter of the sugar mixture evenly onto the dough, then sprinkle on one quarter of the nuts and one quarter of the raisins. Using a pizza cutter or sharp knife, cut across each circle into triangular wedges as you would cut a whole pizza, making at least 12 triangles per circle. Roll up each triangle, starting at the wide end, and place on the cookie sheets, point side down. Repeat with the remaining dough and fillings. Let the rugelach rise for 30 minutes at room temperature. If your house is cold or drafty, cover the rugelach as they rise.

Heat the oven to 375 degrees. Bake the rugelach for 15 to 20 minutes, or until golden brown. Let them cool on wire racks and store in an airtight container for up to 1 week.

tasting trio

Vanilla Snow with Maple Syrup

Fannie's Banana–Blueberry–Sour Cream Salad

Elsie's Baby Rugelach

fig nortons

MAKES ABOUT 65

More than half of the entire American fig crop ends up inside Fig Newtons, one of our enduring cookie classics. Even those who have no fondness for figs will happily munch on the cookies, and you can make even more converts with this easy recipe. My dough has extra crunch and spice to it, which makes a great contrast with the fruity filling. I also put orange juice in the fig mixture to brighten up all the flavors and add apple juice to sweeten it and make it less sticky. We call the result a Fig Norton.

My pastry sous-chef, Megan Kehoe, is a Fig Norton fiend, and she often makes the ones we serve at the restaurant—sometimes alongside an appetizer of *foie gras!*

you'll need

A straightedge or ruler

A large cookie sheet, well greased or lined with parchment paper or with nonstick baking mats (see page 16); or a nonstick cookie sheet

FOR THE DOUGH

3 cups all-purpose flour
½ cup sugar
½ teaspoon salt
¾ teaspoon baking powder
⅜ teaspoon baking soda
½ teaspoon cinnamon
12 tablespoons (1½ sticks) cool unsalted butter, cut into pieces
4 eggs

FOR THE FILLING

1 cup dried figs, cut into ½-inch chunks
½ cup orange juice
½ cup apple juice
¼ teaspoon ground cinnamon

Make the dough: Blend the dry ingredients in a mixer fitted with a paddle attachment (or using a hand mixer). Add the butter and mix at low speed until sandy. Whisk 3 of the eggs together until foamy and add to the bowl. Mix to combine.

Form the dough into a disk, wrap it in plastic wrap, and refrigerate for at least 2 hours.

Make the filling: Combine the ingredients in a saucepan and cook over medium heat until all the liquid is absorbed by the figs and the mixture is thick. Let the mixture cool slightly, then purée it in a food processor (or using a hand blender) until smooth. Refrigerate until ready to bake. *(The recipe can be made up to this point and refrigerated for up to 3 days.)*

When you're ready to bake, heat the oven to 375 degrees. Make an egg wash by whisking the remaining egg with 2 teaspoons of water.

On a lightly floured surface, roll out the dough into a rough rectangle about ⅛ inch thick. Cut the dough lengthwise into strips, at least 2½ inches wide. Paint around the edges of one strip with egg wash. Pipe or spoon the fig filling down the center of the strip and then fold the dough over to enclose the filling, slightly overlapping the long edge. Place the tube, seam side down, on the cookie sheet, then press down lightly to flatten somewhat. Repeat with the remaining dough and filling.

Bake until light golden brown, about 15 minutes. Let the pastries cool to room temperature. Use a sharp knife to cut into 1-inch segments.

tasting trio

Nutmeg Ice Cream with Gingerbread Wafers

Bread Puddings with Orange Marmalade

Fig Nortons

thimble cookies

MAKES 120 TO 150

See photograph, page 147

I felt like the luckiest child in the world when my grandmother Elsie made these for my birthday parties. I remember her skimming that tiny thimble over smooth sheets of cookie dough, rapidly cutting out dozens of the tiniest child-size cookies. There's really only one way to describe them: They are just darling.

Elsie's recipe simply says: Mix all the ingredients, roll, and cut out; and it's almost that easy. The dough naturally produces wonderfully crisp butter–lemon cookies. They are charming when plain, but I also like to divide up the batch and sprinkle the tops with different colored sugars. Pink, purple, green, orange, and blue are festive choices.

If you do not have a thimble, use the end of a large plain pastry tip to cut out the cookies.

you'll need

A thimble or another tiny cutter, such as a pastry-bag tip or the metal top of an olive oil bottle

Two cookie sheets, well greased or lined with parchment paper or with nonstick baking mats (see page 16); or two nonstick cookie sheets

8 ounces (2 sticks) cool unsalted butter, cut into pieces
½ cup sugar
2 egg yolks
½ teaspoon pure vanilla extract
¼ teaspoon freshly grated lemon zest
1 teaspoon freshly squeezed lemon juice
½ teaspoon baking powder
2¼ cups all-purpose flour

Colored sugars of your choice

Cream the butter and sugar in a mixer fitted with a paddle attachment (or using a hand mixer) until smooth. With the mixer running at low speed, add the remaining ingredients (except the colored sugars) and mix until smooth. Form the dough into 2 disks, wrap them separately in plastic, and chill for at least 1 hour. *(The recipe can be made up to this point and kept refrigerated for up to 2 days.)*

When you're ready to bake, heat the oven to 350 degrees. On a lightly floured surface, roll out one disk of dough to a little less than ¼ inch thick.

Using a thimble, and dipping it in flour often to keep the cookies from sticking, cut out tiny rounds of dough. Carefully transfer to the cookie sheets. Reroll the scraps once and cut out more cookies, then discard the scraps (they will become tough if you keep rerolling them).

Sprinkle the tops with plain or colored sugars, then press the sugar lightly into the cookie with your thumbs. Bake until light golden brown, 8 to 10 minutes.

Repeat with the remaining cookie dough. Let the cookies cool on wire racks and store them in an airtight container for up to 1 week.

tasting trio

Chocolate Pots-de-Crème with Orange Whipped Cream

Profiteroles with Caramel Caps

Thimble Cookies

animal crackers

MAKES ABOUT 40

When I ate animal crackers as a child, I always thought that the different animals would be different flavored cookies. But no matter how many boxes I crunched through, they were all exactly the same. Now I have a wonderful set of animal cookie cutters, and I make big batches of animal cookie dough—then divide it up and add seasonings so that the pigs are one kind of cookie, the ducks another, and so on. If only all childhood dreams could be satisfied through baking!

There's no need to stick to animals here; different flowers, snowflakes, dinosaurs, or whatever you have on hand can all be used. I consider these to be the perfect cookie to serve with homemade ice cream because they are mild but not bland, and just a little bit exotic.

you'll need

3 cookie cutters, each one a different shape

Two cookie sheets, well greased or lined with parchment paper or with nonstick baking mats (see page 16); or nonstick cookie sheets

16 tablespoons (2 sticks) cool unsalted butter, cut into pieces
¾ cup sugar
1 egg
¼ teaspoon pure vanilla extract
½ teaspoon baking powder
Scant 3 cups all-purpose flour
2 tablespoons white sesame seeds
1 tablespoon Chinese five-spice powder, or pumpkin pie spice if unavailable
1 tablespoon fennel seed, toasted (see page 12) and crushed

Cream the butter and sugar in a mixer fitted with a paddle attachment (or using a hand mixer) until fluffy. Add the egg and vanilla and mix.

Stir the baking powder and flour together, then add in batches to the butter mixture, mixing just to combine after each addition. Divide the dough into 3 batches. Mix the sesame seeds into one batch, the five-spice powder into another, and the fennel seed into the third, making three different flavored doughs. Form each batch into a disk, wrap separately in plastic, and chill for at least 1 hour. *(The recipe can be made up to this point and kept refrigerated for up to 3 days.)*

When you're ready to bake, heat the oven to 350 degrees.

On a floured surface, roll out the dough to a little less than ¼ inch thick. Cut out cookies, using a different shape for each flavor of cookie. Transfer the cookies to the cookie sheets. Reroll the scraps and cut out more cookies, then discard the scraps (they will become tough if you keep rerolling them).

Bake until golden brown, 10 to 12 minutes. Let the cookies cool on wire racks and store them in an airtight container for up to 1 week.

tasting trio

White-Hot Chocolate

Chocolate Seashells and White Coffee Ice Cream Pearls

Animal Crackers

pecan shortbread bites

MAKES ABOUT 60

Two gloriously rich treats—shortbread and pecans—make this a really luxurious mouthful. The warm, nutty taste of pecans enhances the shortbread, and the shortbread enhances the pecans by wrapping them in a lush "flavor coat" of butter. But it's still a very simple, elemental dessert. Anyone who likes butter pecan ice cream will be mad for this cookie. It's a perfect complement to any fruity, spicy, or chocolaty ice cream, or to just a cup of tea.

you'll need

An 8 x 10-inch baking pan (or smaller), lined with parchment or wax paper

8 tablespoons (1 stick) cool unsalted butter, cut into pieces
¼ cup plus 2 tablespoons sugar
1 cup all-purpose flour
¼ cup cornstarch
¼ teaspoon salt
½ cup chopped pecans, toasted (see page 12) and cooled

Heat the oven to 350 degrees.

Cream the butter until soft in a mixer fitted with a paddle attachment (or using a hand mixer). Add the ¼ cup of sugar and mix until incorporated.

Stir together the flour, cornstarch, and salt in a medium bowl. Add the dry ingredients to the butter mixture and mix at low speed just until the ingredients are almost incorporated, then add the pecans and mix until the dough starts to come together. Flour a work surface, turn the dough onto it, and knead it 5 to 10 times, to bring the dough together and smooth it out.

Reflour your work surface. With a rolling pin, roll out the dough to fit the baking pan. To transfer to the baking pan, roll the dough up onto the rolling pin, lift it up, and unroll into the pan. Using light strokes of the rolling pin, roll the dough into the corners and edges of the pan, and roll out any bumps. (Or, press the dough thoroughly into the pan with your fingers.) Prick the shortbread all over with a fork to prevent any buckling or shrinking. Sprinkle the surface evenly with 1 tablespoon of the remaining sugar.

Bake for 15 minutes. Rotate the pan and deflate the dough by knocking the pan once against the oven rack, to ensure even cooking and a flat surface. Bake 10 to 15 minutes more, until golden all over and very lightly browned. As soon as it comes out of the oven, sprinkle the surface evenly with the remaining tablespoon of sugar. Let the shortbread cool for about 5 minutes.

Using a very sharp knife, cut into 1-inch squares while still warm. Let the shortbread cool completely in the pan. Store in an airtight container for up to 1 week.

tasting trio

Black-and-White Chocolate Mousse Cups

Ruby Raspberry Jellies

Pecan Shortbread Bites

blueberry-stuffed cinnamon shortbread squares

MAKES ABOUT 60

A melting mouthful of buttery shortbread and juicy berries: Who could ask for a better dessert? To make these bites, I layer berry preserves and shortbread dough into a sheet pan, bake the whole thing until golden and crisp, and then cut it into tiny squares.

This is one of the most forgiving, flexible recipes I've ever devised. Grating frozen dough into a pan is so much easier than the usual rolling, and you can use any kind of preserves that takes your fancy. If you're like me, you probably have about a twenty-year supply of different jams in your kitchen—here's a great way to use them up. (Oh, how I love to use things up!) Choose something intense and tart, like a berry or an apricot jam, to contrast with the rich, mild cookie.

8 tablespoons (1 stick) cool unsalted butter, cut into pieces
2 egg yolks
1 cup granulated sugar
2 cups all-purpose flour
1 teaspoon baking powder
½ teaspoon cinnamon
⅛ teaspoon salt
½ cup blueberry preserves, or other preserves of your choice
¼ cup confectioners' sugar

you'll need

A box grater

A small (about 8 x 8-inch) baking dish

Cream the butter in a mixer fitted with a paddle attachment (or using a hand mixer) until soft and fluffy. Add the egg yolks and mix well.

Stir the granulated sugar, flour, baking powder, cinnamon, and salt together in a medium bowl. Add the dry ingredients to the butter mixture and mix at low speed just until the dough starts to come together. Flour a work surface, turn the dough onto it, and knead it 5 to 10 times to bring the dough together and smooth it out. Wrap in plastic wrap and freeze for at least 2 hours. *(The recipe can be made up to this point and kept frozen for up to 1 month. If frozen overnight or longer, let the dough thaw for 30 minutes before continuing.)*

When you're ready to bake, heat the oven to 350 degrees.

Use a box grater to coarsely grate half of the frozen dough into the bottom of the pan. Make sure the surface is covered evenly with shreds of dough.

Use a small offset spatula or the back of a spoon to spread the preserves over the surface, to within ½ inch of the edge all the way around. Coarsely grate the remaining dough over the entire surface, but do not pat it down.

Bake until light golden brown, 25 to 35 minutes. As soon as the shortbread comes out of the oven, sprinkle on all the confectioners' sugar. Cool in the pan on a wire rack, then cut in the pan, using a serrated knife, into 1-inch squares.

tasting trio

Passionate Raspberry Gratins

Coffee Suckers on Cinnamon Sticks

Cinnamon Shortbread Squares

mint–chocolate-chip meringues

MAKES ABOUT 90

See photograph, page 147

Meringues are an absolute classic in the grand tradition of *petit-fours.* But you'll never see a mint–chocolate-chip meringue on a French pastry tray—it's a completely American flavor combination, and one that I love. In this easy, superlight cookie, I use shards of unsweetened chocolate and a sweet meringue mixture for a great contrast.

These meringues do have the melting texture of the French original. But don't expect the bright green color of American mint–chocolate-chip ice cream! The finished meringues are a pale cappuccino color when baked, and they will be dry and crisp all the way through to the center.

you'll need

A pastry bag (optional; see page 15), fitted with a large plain tip

Two cookie sheets, well greased or lined with parchment paper or with nonstick baking mats (see page 16); or nonstick cookie sheets

½ cup egg whites (from about 4 eggs)
⅔ cup sugar
½ teaspoon mint extract or mint flavoring (*not* mint oil)
2 ounces unsweetened chocolate, finely chopped or grated
2 ounces semisweet chocolate

Heat the oven to 325 degrees.

Warm the egg whites and sugar in the top of a double boiler set over barely simmering water until warm to the touch (this will help you get more air into the whites when you whip them). Transfer to a mixer fitted with a whisk attachment and whip until stiff and glossy. Add the mint extract and continue whipping just until incorporated, about 10 seconds. Fold in the chopped unsweetened chocolate.

Scrape the mixture into the pastry bag. Pipe bite-size kisses in rows onto the cookie sheets and bake until the meringues are the color of milky coffee, 25 to 30 minutes. To test, remove a meringue from the oven, let it cool for

1 minute, then taste. It should be dry and crisp all the way through. Let the meringues cool on the pans.

Melt the semisweet chocolate (see page 11). Dipping the tines of a fork into the chocolate, drizzle the meringues with melted chocolate. Let them sit until the chocolate is set, 30 minutes to an hour (or let them set in the refrigerator for 15 minutes).

Store in an airtight container at room temperature for up to 3 days.

tasting trio

Brittle-Topped Vanilla–Butterscotch Pudding Parfaits

Vanilla-Crusted Strawberries

Meringues

stained-glass cookies

MAKES 30 TO 40

See photograph, page 145

After you pour the candy syrup into these blonde-baked sugar cookies, you'll understand the name completely. This is a visually irresistible cookie treat, with clear, bright-colored candy centers: pink hearts, orange initials, blue stars, or whatever combination of cookie cutter and food coloring you dream up. They sound like they're just for kids, but the results can be surprisingly elegant, especially if you don't overdo it on the food coloring. A pale-peach candy initial set into a buttery cookie makes a lovely personalized treat. Eat the cookie part first, then pop the candy.

you'll need

- 1 large (about 2½-inch) and 1 small (about 1-inch) cookie cutter, heart shape or any shape you like
- Two cookie sheets, well greased or lined with parchment paper or with nonstick baking mats (see page 16); or nonstick cookie sheets
- A candy thermometer

FOR THE COOKIES

½ cup sugar
6 tablespoons cool unsalted butter, cut into pieces
⅓ cup vegetable shortening
1 egg yolk
⅛ teaspoon pure vanilla extract
¼ teaspoon baking powder
1¾ cups all-purpose flour

FOR THE CANDY CENTERS

1 cup sugar
3 tablespoons light corn syrup
A few drops of food coloring, any color
¼ teaspoon pure almond, orange, or lemon extract (see Sources, page 300)

Make the cookies: Cream the sugar, butter, and shortening until fluffy in a mixer fitted with a paddle attachment (or using a hand mixer). Add the yolk, vanilla, and baking powder and mix. Add the flour and mix. Shape the dough into a large flat disk, kneading briefly if necessary to bring the dough together. Wrap in plastic wrap and refrigerate for 1 to 2 hours.

Heat the oven to 350 degrees. On a lightly floured surface, roll out the dough to ¼ inch thick. Use the large cookie cutter to cut out cookies about 2½ inches in diameter. Transfer to the cookie sheets.

Using the small cookie cutter, cut a circle (or another shape of your choice) out of the center of each cookie (to later pour the candy centers into). Bake the cookies until light golden, 15 to 20 minutes. Let them cool completely on the pan.

Make the candy centers: Combine the sugar, corn syrup, and ½ cup water in a clean, dry, small saucepan (preferably one with a pouring spout) fitted with the candy thermometer and bring to a boil over high heat. Without stirring, cook until the mixture reaches 305 degrees, or "hard-crack" stage on the candy thermometer. (While the syrup is cooking, occasionally wash down the sides of the pan with a clean brush dipped in water, to prevent crystallization.)

Half-fill a large bowl with ice and add cold water to cover. When the syrup reaches 305 degrees, remove the pot from the heat and dip the bottom into the ice water for 15 seconds to stop the cooking. Remove the pot from the ice water and add the color and extract, stirring very gently in both directions with a wooden spoon (this will help eliminate air bubbles in the finished centers). Do not mix more than absolutely necessary.

Gently pour or ladle the syrup into the cutouts until just barely full. Set aside to cool for at least 30 minutes, or until hard. Gently lift the cookies from the pans, using a spatula if necessary to loosen them. Store in an airtight container for up to 1 week (less in very humid weather).

tasting trio

Double-Vanilla Crème Brûleés

Frozen Cream–Dark Chocolate Sandwiches

Stained-Glass Cookies

orange tuiles

MAKES 25 TO 30

See photograph, page 147

Crisp, melting tuiles—thin confections of sugar and butter barely bound together—hover somewhere between candy and cookies and can lean in either direction depending on how much flour is used. Tuiles can be as brittle-crisp as the glassy top of a crème brûlée, or, like these, as delicate as the ghost of a butter cookie.

These sunny tuiles sing with texture and flavor from flaked coconut and orange zest, with a bass note of almonds. Don't worry if the edges are a bit rough and crumbly; the important thing is to spread the batter as thin as possible. You can make them well in advance and store them in an airtight container. Feel free to spread the finished cookies with melted dark chocolate and make sandwiches, if you prefer.

you'll need

Two cookie sheets, lined with parchment paper or with nonstick baking mats (see page 16)

1 cup blanched almonds, whole or slivered
1¼ cups plus 2 tablespoons sugar
7 tablespoons cool unsalted butter, cut into pieces
7 tablespoons orange juice, preferably freshly squeezed
3 tablespoons Grand Marnier or another orange liqueur
7 tablespoons all-purpose flour
5 tablespoons flaked or shredded coconut, finely chopped

Put the almonds and all of the sugar in a food processor and pulse together just until the mixture is sandy looking. Stop often to let the machine cool down and to check the consistency; overprocessing will make the mixture pasty.

Cream the butter until fluffy in a mixer fitted with a paddle attachment (or using a hand mixer). Add the almond–sugar mixture and continue mixing until smooth. At low speed, mix in the orange juice and liqueur. Add the flour and coconut and mix just until combined. *(The recipe can be made up to this point and kept refrigerated for up to 4 days.)*

Heat the oven to 350 degrees. Drop teaspoonfuls of batter in rows on the cookie sheets, leaving about 3 inches between the cookies. Dip a fork into lukewarm water and use the back of the tines to flatten each cookie out into a round about 2 inches across. They should be very thin, so that you can almost see the pan through the cookie.

Bake in the center of the oven until golden brown, 10 to 12 minutes. Let the tuiles cool on the pan, then carefully remove with a spatula. Store in an airtight container for up to 3 days.

If you want to make curved tuiles (like the photograph), remove the tuiles while they are still hot and drape them over a rolling pin. Let them cool, then store.

tasting trio

Pecan-Crusted Goat Cheese with Quince Compote

Pineapple and Melon Ball Brochettes

Orange Tuiles

french macaroons with coffee cream

MAKES ABOUT 36

See photograph, page 147

French macaroons are light, crisp, and altogether different from our chewy macaroons. They are made from almonds, not coconut, and in France they are colored delicate shades of green, pink, and brown. On display in bakery cases, they glow like pastel jewels.

The best French macaroons I have ever tasted were made by Roland and Mary Beth Liccioni of Les Nomades. The crispness makes them wonderful, with a rich buttercream frosting.

you'll need

A pastry bag fitted with a ¼-inch plain tip

A large cookie sheet, lined with parchment paper or with nonstick baking mats (see page 16); or a nonstick cookie sheet

clothespin

FOR THE COOKIES

1½ cups confectioners' sugar
⅞ cup almond flour (available at gourmet and health-food stores) or ground almonds
Scant ½ cup egg whites (from 3 to 4 eggs)
2 tablespoons granulated sugar

FOR THE COFFEE CREAM

8 tablespoons (1 stick) unsalted butter, at room temperature
¼ cup confectioners' sugar
1½ teaspoons hot water
¾ teaspoon instant coffee
¼ teaspoon pure vanilla extract

Make the cookies: Heat the oven to 300 degrees. Stir the confectioners' sugar and almond flour together. Sift the mixture through a mesh strainer to remove any chunks of almond.

Whip the egg whites until frothy in a mixer fitted with a whisk attachment. Add the granulated sugar and whip until stiff. Gently fold in a third of the almond mixture; the mixture should stay streaky. Add another third and fold very lightly. Add the final third and fold the mixture until combined, leaving a few specks of egg whites. The batter will be rather soupy.

Place the pastry bag (with a clothespin holding it shut at the bottom) in a tall round container such as a coffee can, mayonnaise jar, or vase, folding the edge of the bag over the rim of the container to fill it easily.

Pipe rows of kisses 1 inch in diameter (about the size of a quarter), ½ inch apart on the cookie sheets. Bake for about 17 minutes, rotating the pans after 8 minutes, until very light brown.

While the cookies are still hot, remove the meringues from the parchment by spooning a tablespoon of water under each edge of the paper. This will steam the cookies loose. Let cool and peel off.

Meanwhile, make the coffee cream: Whip the butter until very light and fluffy in a mixer fitted with a whisk attachment, scraping down the bowl often to make sure that all the butter is whipped. Add the confectioners' sugar and mix at low speed. Combine the hot water and the coffee and let dissolve. Drizzle in the coffee and vanilla and mix to combine. Transfer to a clean pastry bag fitted with a large or small plain tip.

Make sandwiches by piping a ⅛-inch layer of coffee cream onto the flat sides of half of the cookies. Lightly press the flat sides of the unfrosted cookies to the frosted ones. Refrigerate in an airtight container for up to 3 days.

tasting trio

Ruby Raspberry Jellies

Orange–Cardamom Chocolate Truffles

French Macaroons with Coffee Cream

Stellar Apple Spice Cakes ◎ Butterfly Cupcakes

Coconut Snowballs ◎ Twinkle Twinkles

Peachy Upside-Down Cakes

Devil's Peaks with Double-Chocolate Drizzle

Blackberry Brown-Butter Financiers ◎ Chockablock

Chocolate Cakes with Warm Macadamia Nut Caramel

Tiny Lemon Angel Cakes with Lemon Confit

Cranberry–Walnut Crumb Cakes

Frozen Creamy Dark Chocolate Sandwiches

Cannelés (Slow-Baked French Vanilla Cakes)

Saffron Madeleines ◎ Tangerine Marmalade Babycakes

Very Red Velvet Cupcakes ◎ Pound Cake Tea Sandwiches

Sour Cream Seed Cakes with Earl Grey Glaze

cake BITES

stellar apple spice cakes

MAKES 24

My mother, Myrna, and her best friend, Stella, always reminded me of Betty Rubble and Wilma Flintstone. One dark, one fair, they lived about thirty yards apart but spent hours on the phone each day. Both of them were terrific bakers with two kids, so the households often traded desserts back and forth.

My mother's repertoire was mostly Austro-Hungarian, but Stella had lived in Montreal and knew a lot of French pastries, which impressed me tremendously. The first miniature tartlet I ever ate was baked by Stella, and she kindly made an enormous number of them for my wedding. But my father always thought that this homey cake, loaded with fruit, was Stella's best recipe.

you'll need

1 or 2 Bundt muffin tins (makes mini-Bundt cakes with no hole) or regular muffin tins, buttered and floured (or use nonstick)

FOR THE CAKE

1 cup chopped dates or whole raisins (dark or golden)
2 cups all-purpose flour
3 eggs
1½ cups sugar
1 cup vegetable oil
1 teaspoon pure vanilla extract
1 teaspoon salt
1 teaspoon baking soda
1 teaspoon cinnamon
½ teaspoon ground cloves
½ teaspoon ground allspice
2 cups peeled apple chunks (from about 3 apples)
1 cup chopped walnuts

FOR THE GLAZE

½ cup maple syrup
1½ cups confectioners' sugar

Heat the oven to 350 degrees. Place the dates or raisins in a bowl and toss them with 2 tablespoons of the flour until lightly coated (this will prevent them from sinking in the cake batter during baking).

Beat the eggs and sugar in a mixer fitted with a whisk attachment (or using a hand mixer) until fluffy. With the mixer running, slowly pour in the oil and vanilla. In a separate bowl, mix together the flour, salt, baking soda, cinnamon, cloves, and allspice. Mix into the egg mixture. Mix in the apples and nuts, then stir in the dates or raisins by hand, distributing them evenly in the batter. Spoon into the muffin tins and bake about 35 minutes, until springy and dry in the center. Let the cakes cool in the tins on a wire rack, then turn out.

Meanwhile, make the glaze: Stir the maple syrup and confectioners' sugar together in a bowl. Glaze the cooled cakes by spooning the glaze around the tops of the cakes and letting it drip down the sides.

tasting trio

Maytag Blue Grapes

Nutmeg Ice Cream with Gingerbread Wafers

Stellar Apple Spice Cakes

butterfly cupcakes

MAKES 12

See photograph, page 149

Here's proof that there is something even cuter than a cupcake. Princess Diana's butler, Paul Burrell, taught me to slice off the cupcake's cap, cut it in half, and turn it into the colorful wings of a butterfly. He made these on the Princes' birthdays, as part of the boys' bug theme party—complete with a big ladybug cake and cheese pastries coiled up like snails, with antennae made of chives. I make them for *my* prince's birthdays: My son, Gio, loves them.

you'll need

A muffin tin

12 ribbed paper cupcake liners

FOR THE CUPCAKES

1¼ cups sifted cake flour
½ teaspoon baking soda
¼ teaspoon baking powder
¼ teaspoon salt
8 tablespoons (1 stick) cool unsalted butter, cut into pieces
½ cup plus 2 tablespoons sugar
1 egg yolk
1 egg
1 teaspoon pure vanilla extract
½ cup sour cream

FOR THE DECORATING

White frosting from Very Red Velvet Cupcakes (page 96) or another white frosting of your choice
Rainbow sprinkles
12 2-inch lengths of red licorice whips or Twizzlers
12 1½-inch lengths of black licorice whips
1 tube of black icing (the supermarket kind with a small writing tip)

Line the muffin tin with the cupcake liners. Heat the oven to 350 degrees.

Sift the sifted flour with the baking soda, baking powder, and salt.

Cream the butter in a mixer fitted with a whisk attachment until soft, then add the sugar and mix at medium-high speed until light and fluffy. Add the yolk and the egg and mix, then add the vanilla and combine.

With the mixer running at low speed, add a third of the flour mixture and mix. Then add half of the sour cream and mix. Add another third of the flour and mix. Add the remaining sour cream and mix, then the remaining flour. Give it one last mix to make sure everything is blended in.

Pour the batter into the muffin cups, filling them three-fourths full. Bake until firm to the touch in the center, 20 to 25 minutes. Set the pan on a wire rack and let the cupcakes cool.

When the cupcakes have cooled, make the butterflies: Spread a thick layer of rainbow sprinkles on a plate.

Cut off the top rounded "cap" (like the cap of a mushroom or a muffin) of each cupcake. Spread the flat top of each "beheaded" cupcake with frosting

Spread the cut side of each cap with frosting, then dip in rainbow sprinkles to coat. To make the wings, cut a V shape out of each cap, down the center to cut the cap in half. Turn the wing pieces over so they are sprinkles side up and place on top of each cupcake so they angle up like wings (see photograph).

Lay a piece of red licorice down the center of each one to make the body (3 pieces if using thin licorice). Use two pieces of black licorice to make the antennae. Pipe two black dots for the eyes, placing one white sprinkle in the center of each eye.

coconut snowballs

MAKES 12 TO 24

See photograph, page 150

Each of these fluffy, pure-white cakes looks like a hand-packed snowball. Flaked coconut gives the outsides just the right feathery texture. Inside, the tender white cake lightly flavored with vanilla, almond, and lemon is fabulously light.

This stiff white frosting comes from the classic *Settlement Cookbook,* but you can use any white frosting you like. If you would like to add color to the dessert, toss the coconut thoroughly with a few drops of food coloring; it takes on color very well.

you'll need

12 dome-shaped baking molds (about 4-ounce capacity) or a regular or mini-muffin tin, buttered and floured or sprayed with nonstick cooking spray and floured

FOR THE CAKES

4 egg whites (½ cup)
8 tablespoons (1 stick) cool unsalted butter
1 cup sugar
½ teaspoon pure vanilla extract
½ teaspoon pure almond extract
Freshly grated zest of 1 lemon
2 cups sifted cake flour
1 tablespoon baking powder
⅔ cup milk

FOR THE FROSTING

2 egg whites
6 tablespoons cold water
1½ cups sugar
½ teaspoon cream of tartar
1 teaspoon pure vanilla extract

2 cups sweetened shredded or flaked coconut
Food coloring (optional; see above)

In a mixer fitted with a whisk attachment (or using a hand mixer), whip the egg whites until stiff but not dry. Refrigerate.

Heat the oven to 350 degrees.

In a mixer fitted with a paddle attachment (or using a hand mixer), cream the butter until smooth. With the mixer running, slowly add the sugar and mix. Add the vanilla, almond extract, and lemon zest and mix well.

Sift the flour 3 times with the baking powder (this is to lighten the cakes). Add a third of the flour mixture to the butter mixture and mix. Add half of the milk to the butter mixture and mix. Add another third of the flour mixture and mix. Add the remaining milk and mix. Add the remaining flour and mix until smooth. Fold in the egg whites.

Pour the batter into the prepared molds, filling them about three-fourths full. Bake until the cakes are firm to the touch and almost dry in the center, 20 to 25 minutes. Let them cool in the pan.

Make the frosting: Off the heat, combine the egg whites, cold water, sugar, and cream of tartar in the top of a double boiler. Whisk until smooth. Place over boiling water and whisk constantly or beat with a hand mixer until the frosting is stiff and holds peaks (this will take 10 to 15 minutes). Remove from the heat and whisk in the vanilla. Let the frosting cool, whisking often.

Put the coconut in a bowl and add just a few drops of food coloring. Wearing clean rubber gloves, toss well. If desired, add more coloring and repeat.

Turn out the cakes so that the flat top of each cake becomes the bottom. You want the cakes to rest flat, so you may need to cut a thin slice off.

Frost the rounded top and sides of each cake. Roll each one in coconut to make it look like a snowball. Sprinkle any leftover coconut on a platter, arrange the cakes on top, and serve.

tasting trio

Roasted Strawberries with Cherry Balsamic Sauce

Hot Cocoa Shots

Coconut Snowballs

twinkle twinkles

MAKES ABOUT 18

Somewhere deep inside all of us, there seems to be a universal urge to eat golden yellow sponge cake with fluffy whipped-cream filling. The combination is lush and irresistible, even if you haven't tried it in a long time. Unlike commercial versions, these cream-stuffed fingers of cake are wholesome and bright tasting. They're also very easy to make.

you'll need

- A 9 x 13-inch baking pan
- Parchment or wax paper (see page 16)
- An apple corer
- A pastry bag, fitted with a small plain tip (optional; see page 15)
- About 18 ribbed paper cupcake liners

FOR THE CAKE

1½ cups cake flour
1½ teaspoons baking powder
½ teaspoon salt
¾ cup milk
3 tablespoons unsalted butter
1 tablespoon pure vanilla extract
3 eggs
1¼ cups sugar

FOR THE FILLING

1 cup chilled heavy cream
½ teaspoon pure vanilla extract
1 tablespoon sugar

Line the baking pan with parchment paper. Heat the oven to 350 degrees.

Make the cake: Combine the flour, baking powder, and salt in a large bowl. Sift together three times.

Combine the milk and butter in a saucepan and bring to a boil. Turn off the heat and add the vanilla extract. Combine the eggs and sugar in a mixer fitted with a whisk attachment (or using a hand mixer) and beat until light and fluffy. With the mixer running, drizzle in the hot milk. Gradually fold in the sifted dry ingredients just until combined. Pour the batter into the pan, smooth the top, and bake until the cake feels springy to the touch, 20 to 25 minutes.

Set the pan on a wire rack and let the cake cool in the pan. Turn the cake out onto a work surface, with the long side running horizontal to your body, and peel off the parchment paper. Chill the cake fingers for at least 1 hour to make them easier to cut and fill.

Cut the cake in half lengthwise, then crosswise into fingers, making them as wide as they are thick. (For example, if your cake is 1½ inches thick, the fingers should be 1½ inches wide). This should give you about 18 squared-off fingers of cake, about 4½ × 1½ × 1½ inches.

Using the apple corer, make a tunnel down the center of each cake finger, reserving the cut-out cake pieces.

Make the filling: Whip the cream, vanilla, and sugar in a medium bowl until stiff, and transfer to the pastry bag fitted with a small plain tip.

Pipe the cream into each cake, then plug the ends with ½-inch-long pieces of reserved cake. Chill until ready to serve. The twinkles may sit out at room temperature for 1 hour.

To serve, flatten out the paper cupcake liners until they lie flat. Place the twinkles on them and fold the edges up around the sides.

tasting trio

Raspberry Smallovers

Chocolate–Mint Tiddlywinks

Twinkle Twinkles

peachy upside-down cakes

MAKES 10

Upside-down cake is all about the simple combination of juicy fruit and fluffy cake, and to me the velvety texture of baked peach slices is the absolute best. (Yes, I prefer peach to pineapple here!) When you turn each little treat out of the pan, the peach-and-brown-sugar syrup melts deliciously down into the cake. A few nuggets of dried cherry provide extra tang and texture.

1 cup apple juice
½ cup dried cherries
2 peaches
12 tablespoons (1½ sticks) cool unsalted butter
1 cup (packed) dark brown sugar
1 cup cake flour
1½ teaspoons baking powder
Pinch of salt
1 vanilla bean, halved lengthwise, insides scraped out with the point of a sharp knife and reserved
1 cup granulated sugar
2 eggs
6 tablespoons whole milk

you'll need

A muffin tin or 10 ramekins (see page 19)

Bring the apple juice to a boil in a small pot, add the cherries, and turn off the heat. Stir well and let soak until tender, at least 20 minutes. Drain well, reserving the soaking liquid, and chop the cherries coarsely.

Meanwhile, cut the peaches in half, remove the stones, then slice into thin wedges (about ¼-inch thick) and set aside. Melt 6 tablespoons of the butter and divide it among 10 muffin cups, then sprinkle the cups evenly with the brown sugar. Arrange 2 peach wedges in each cup, facing each other to make a circle that covers the bottom completely.

Heat the oven to 350 degrees.

Sift the flour, baking powder, and salt together three times. Cream the remaining 6 tablespoons of butter, the vanilla scrapings, and the granulated sugar together in a mixer fitted with a whisk attachment (or use a hand mixer). One at a time, add the eggs and mix until fluffy. Add a third of the dry ingredients and mix. Add half of the milk and mix. Add another third of the dry ingredients and mix. Add the remaining milk and the reserved cherry soaking liquid and mix. Add the remaining dry ingredients and mix just until smooth. Fold in the cherries.

Pour the batter into the cups. Bake until a cake tester comes out clean, 20 to 25 minutes. Let the cakes cool for 5 minutes, then run a butter knife around the sides of the cups. Quickly invert the pan onto a work surface. Transfer the cakes to serving plates and serve warm.

tasting trio

Toasted Coconut Risotto with Pecans

Crunchy Chocolate Haystacks

Peachy Upside-Down Cakes

devil's peaks with double-chocolate drizzle

MAKES 12

See photograph, page 151

I love these perfectly pointed little cones of devil's food cake. I was in my kitchen one day working through this recipe, trying to figure out a home-kitchen substitute for the cone-shaped baking molds I use. As usual, I got up to pace and think—and my eyes went straight to the water cooler and its tiny cups. In a minute, I had buttered them, filled them with batter, and popped them into the oven. They work just like cupcake or muffin paper liners; just peel off and serve. You must make sure to butter them all the way down into the points, using a small pastry brush, or the tops of the peaks will be lost. Of course, these cakes are moist, dark, and delicious no matter what shape they are.

I like to serve these on a dark-colored plate dusted with confectioners' sugar, to look like snow. Set them on chocolate cookie bases to make witches' hats for a Halloween party.

you'll need

- 12 small paper cone cups (the kind that come with a spring-water cooler), buttered all the way into the points
- 12 squares of aluminum foil, about 12 x 12 inches
- A muffin tin

FOR THE CAKE

- 8 tablespoons (1 stick) unsalted butter, at room temperature
- 1½ cups (packed) light brown sugar
- 2 eggs
- 1 teaspoon pure vanilla extract
- 6 tablespoons cocoa powder
- 1½ teaspoons baking soda
- ¼ teaspoon salt
- 1½ cups sifted cake flour
- ⅔ cup sour cream
- ¾ cup hot coffee

FOR THE TOPPING

- 4 ounces milk chocolate, melted (see page 11)
- 4 ounces white chocolate, melted (see page 11)

Holding one square of foil, rest the pointed base of a cone into the center and gather the foil square up around the cone. Then fold down the corners of the square, scrunching up the foil to make a holder that will prop the cone up as it bakes. Repeat with the remaining foil squares. Arrange the holders in the cups of the muffin tin.

Heat the oven to 350 degrees.

Make the cake: Cream the butter and sugar until smooth in a mixer fitted with a whisk attachment. Add the eggs and mix until fluffy, about 3 minutes. Add the vanilla, cocoa, baking soda, and salt and mix. Add a third of the flour, then half of the sour cream, and mix. Add another third of the flour and the remaining sour cream and mix. Add the remaining flour and mix. Drizzle in the hot coffee and mix until smooth. The batter will be thin.

Pour the batter into the cones, filling them to within ½ inch of the top. Rest each filled paper cone in a holder and bake until the tops are firm to the touch and a toothpick inserted into the center comes out clean (a few crumbs are okay), 20 to 25 minutes. Let the cakes cool in the cones for 30 minutes.

If any of the cones overflowed during baking, trim the tops flat, using a serrated knife and a sawing motion.

Carefully peel off the paper cones to reveal the cakes and invert them onto a wire rack set over parchment paper, points sticking up. If you have to re-trim the bottoms to make the cakes stand up, use a serrated knife and a sawing motion.

Apply the topping: Using forks to dip into the melted chocolate, drizzle both kinds of chocolate over each peak in thin lines. Let the chocolate set at room temperature or, if you're in a hurry, in the refrigerator.

tasting trio

Parfaits of Tangerine Sorbet and Sour-Cream Ice Cream

French Macaroons with Coffee Cream

Devil's Peaks

blackberry brown-butter financiers

MAKES
20 TO 40

I think of *financiers* as a French "newlywed" dessert, a delicious basic that you learn to make when you're just starting out and that will serve you well forever. I learned financiers in my very first week of pastry school at La Varenne in Paris, and I haven't gone a week without baking them since. At my restaurant we make them every day for the *petit-four* trays, changing the ripe fruit to suit the season.

Financiers are simply buttery sponge cakes, with a scoop of almond flour added for moistness and flavor. They are the perfect base for tangy fruits that don't need much enhancement, such as berries. If you have never made brown butter, or *beurre noisette* ("hazelnut butter"), you'll be amazed at how it adds to the nutty, toasty flavor of the finished dessert.

Using almond flour, which is available at gourmet and health-food stores, will give you a paler, finer cake, as it is made from blanched almonds. But you can use supermarket ground almonds; the flavor will still be excellent, though the color will be darker. The applesauce in the recipe keeps the cakes extra moist.

you'll need

- A pastry bag (optional; see page 15) with large plain tip
- 2 mini-muffin tins, or about 40 small baking molds (see page 18), thickly buttered

9 tablespoons (1 stick plus 1 tablespoon) unsalted butter, at room temperature
½ cup almond flour or ground almonds (see above)
1 cup confectioners' sugar, plus extra for sprinkling
¼ cup plus 2 tablespoons all-purpose flour
½ cup egg whites (from about 4 eggs)
1 teaspoon applesauce
About 20 large blackberries, or other berries of your choice

Make the brown butter: Melt the butter in a saucepan over medium heat. The butter will separate into melted golden fat and white, grainy milk solids. Keep cooking until the milk solids turn golden brown and the mixture smells

like toasted nuts, making beurre noisette. Let the butter cool slightly, then strain it through a fine strainer to remove the toasted milk solids.

Sift the dry ingredients together and transfer to a mixer fitted with a whip attachment. Add the egg whites, applesauce, and strained beurre noisette and mix. *(The recipe can be made up to this point and kept refrigerated for up to 3 days.)*

When ready to bake, heat the oven to 375 degrees. Cut the blackberries in half, from top to bottom.

Pipe or spoon the batter into the prepared pans, filling them three-quarters full. Place half of a blackberry in the center of each mold, cut side down. Bake for 10 to 12 minutes, or until golden and browned around the edges.

Let the cakes cool in the molds, then gently lift them out. Sprinkle with confectioners' sugar and serve.

tasting trio

Lemon Cream Daisies

Sugar-Frosted Frozen Grapes

Blackberry Brown-Butter Financiers

chockablock chocolate cakes with warm macadamia nut caramel

MAKES 12 TO 24 SERVINGS

See photograph, page 152

Hands down, this is the most popular chocolate dessert I've ever served.

German chocolate cake—mild cake layered with coconut caramel—is a classic, but I always thought it could stand to be more intense, nuttier, and less sweet. So my then-assistant Martha and I developed a powerfully chocolatey cake batter with a dark chocolate edge. Then I toasted the coconut and added macadamia to the topping. Now it's an extreme version of the original: velvety dark cake, with a warm sticky topping full of crunch and nuts. The way it all combines in your mouth is spectacular.

You'll be making a big sheet of cake, then cutting it out into rounds for individual servings. Don't worry about what to do with the leftover scraps of cake; you'll find plenty of takers. I substitute them for the bread in my favorite chocolate bread pudding recipe. You can freeze the scraps to use later, if you aren't ready for another irresistible indulgence right away.

you'll need

A baking pan with sides, about 9 x 13 inches

Parchment or wax paper

A 1½- to 2-inch round biscuit or cookie cutter

FOR THE CAKE

3 cups sugar
2¾ cups all-purpose flour
1⅛ cups cocoa powder, preferably Dutch-processed
2¼ teaspoons baking powder
2¼ teaspoons baking soda
1½ teaspoons salt
3 eggs
1½ cups milk
¾ cup vegetable oil
1 tablespoon pure vanilla extract
1½ cups very hot water

FOR THE CARAMEL

1¼ cups sugar
⅔ cup heavy cream
½ cup macadamia nuts, toasted (see page 12) and roughly chopped
½ cup flaked sweetened coconut, toasted (see page 12)

Heat the oven to 350 degrees. Grease the sheet pan and line the bottom and sides with parchment or wax paper.

Make the cake: Sift together the sugar, flour, cocoa, baking powder, baking soda, and salt. Transfer to a mixer fitted with a whisk attachment (or use a hand mixer) and blend briefly.

Whisk together the eggs, milk, oil, and vanilla extract in a medium bowl. Add to the dry ingredients and mix at low speed for 5 minutes. Gradually add the hot water, mixing at low speed just until combined. The batter will be quite thin.

Pour the batter into the pan. Bake until a tester inserted in the center of the cake comes out clean (a few crumbs are okay) and the center feels firm to the touch, 25 to 35 minutes. Let the cake cool in the pan. Chill, covered, until ready to cut the cake.

Meanwhile, make the caramel: Pour the sugar into the center of a deep saucepan. Carefully pour ⅓ cup water around the walls of the pan, trying not to splash any sugar onto the walls. Do not stir; gently draw your finger twice through the center of the sugar, making a cross, to moisten it. Over high heat, bring to a full boil and cook without stirring, swirling the pan occasionally to even out the color, until the mixture is medium caramel in color, 5 to

recipe continues on next page

10 minutes. Immediately turn off the heat and use a wooden spoon to slowly and carefully stir in the cream (it will bubble up and may splatter). Stir in the macadamia nuts and coconut. Set aside.

When ready to serve, cut rounds of the chilled cake with the biscuit or cookie cutter. If the cake seems to be sticking, dip the cutter in cocoa powder between cuts.

If the sauce has cooled, rewarm it over low heat (or in a microwave) until softened. Place a cake (or two) on each plate, and drizzle with caramel sauce.

tasting trio

Parfaits of Tangerine Sorbet and Sour-Cream Ice Cream

Meringue Cigarettes

Chockablock Chocolate Cakes

tiny lemon angel cakes with lemon confit

MAKES ABOUT 24

See photograph, page 153

A triple play on lemon—my favorite dessert flavor. First, you bake freshly grated lemon zest into a tiny, fluffy angel food cake, giving it just a wisp of flavor. Then you add juice to a simple icing for a sweet-and-sour effect. Last, you candy the lemon rind into a concentrated, almost chewy hit of pure lemon and sugar to use as a final garnish. And even with all this complexity, there isn't a speck of fat in the dessert.

Using acids like lemon juice, vinegar, or cream of tartar (as I do here) is common in recipes that include whipped egg whites. That's because those acids encourage the egg whites to foam up and combine with the air you're whipping in, giving structure and volume to the cake.

you'll need

Pastry bag, optional (see page 15) with a large plain tip

1 large or 2 small mini-muffin tins (see page 18), ungreased

FOR THE CONFIT

2 large lemons
1 cup granulated sugar

FOR THE CAKE

1⅛ cups sifted cake flour
1½ cups granulated sugar
1½ cups egg whites (from about 12 eggs), preferably at room temperature
1¼ teaspoons cream of tartar
½ teaspoon salt
Freshly grated zest of 1 lemon
1 teaspoon pure vanilla extract

FOR THE GLAZE

¼ cup freshly squeezed lemon juice
1½ cups confectioners' sugar

recipe continues on next page

Make the confit: Cut a slice off the top and bottom of each lemon to expose the flesh. Cutting from top to bottom and following the contours of the fruit, cut off the peel and white pith in 1-inch-wide strips. Scrape off any pulp adhering to the strips, but leave the pith intact.

You now have several 1-inch-wide strips of lemon peel and pith. Cut each one into long strips, about ¼-inch by 3 inches each.

Meanwhile, boil a kettleful of water. Pour about 2 cups of the boiling water into a small saucepan, bring back to a boil, add all the lemon rind, and boil for 30 seconds. Drain in a strainer and rinse the rind under cold running water. Repeat 2 times more, using fresh boiling water each time.

Combine the sugar and 2 cups of tap water in the saucepan and bring to a boil. Add the blanched rind and reduce the heat to a simmer. Simmer the rind until tender, about 1 hour. Drain the rind in a strainer (reserve the sweet, lemony syrup for sweetening drinks, if you like). Arrange the strips on a wire rack, using your fingers to gently spread them out so that they do not touch each other. Let them cool and store them in an airtight container.

Make the cake: Heat the oven to 375 degrees.

Sift the sifted cake flour with ½ cup of the sugar 3 times (this is to aerate the mixture and make it lighter). Set aside.

Whip the egg whites in a mixer fitted with a whisk attachment until foamy. Add the cream of tartar and salt and continue whipping until soft peaks form. With the mixer running, gradually add the remaining cup of sugar and continue whipping until the whites are stiff and the sugar is dissolved, about 30 seconds more.

Fold the sifted flour–sugar mixture into the whites by hand just until incorporated. Fold in the lemon zest and vanilla extract.

Spoon or pipe the batter into the cups of the ungreased mini-muffin tin, filling the cups until almost full (they will not expand much). Bake until the cakes are light golden brown, 12 to 16 minutes.

Let the cakes cool in the tin, then run a butter knife around the edges to cut the cakes free, leaving the browned walls and bottom of the cake in the pan. Remove the cakes from the tin and place on a wire rack set over a sheet pan.

Finish the dessert: Stir the glaze ingredients together until smooth. Turn the cakes over so the brown top becomes the base. Dip the new top (the white side) of each cake into the glaze, then carefully place it on the wire rack, glaze side up, to set.

Chop the lemon confit (you may not need all of it) and make a little mound of chopped confit in the center of each cake. Let the glaze set for 30 minutes before serving the cakes.

tasting trio

Cherry Charlottes

Cinnamon Peanut Brittle

Tiny Lemon Angel Cakes with Lemon Confit

cranberry–walnut crumb cakes

MAKES 40 TO 60

These sunny, seductive little cakes are perfect mouthfuls of coffeecake—from the golden crumb to the zingy cranberry bits to the browned, chunky topping that crumbles apart in your mouth. A basket of these is equally good for breakfast, for teatime, or as an autumn dessert.

All the old baking books in my collection include recipe after recipe for coffee cake. Back then, the mid-morning coffee break—a stimulating cup and a bite of something sweet—was a given. Don't we still deserve a little treat to get us through the rest of the day?

Everything about the recipe can be done in advance, right down to filling the cups with batter. Just don't sprinkle on the topping (which you can make literally months in advance and keep in the freezer) until just before you bake.

you'll need

2 mini-muffin tins or 40 small baking molds (see page 18)

Ribbed paper cupcake liners (optional)

FOR THE CAKES

8 tablespoons (1 stick) unsalted butter, at room temperature
1 cup granulated sugar
3 eggs
2 cups sifted all-purpose flour
1 teaspoon baking soda
1 teaspoon baking powder
¼ teaspoon salt
1 cup sour cream
½ cup dried cranberries, cherries, or raisins

FOR THE TOPPING

¾ cup (packed) light brown sugar
1 tablespoon all-purpose flour
1 teaspoon cinnamon
2 tablespoons cold unsalted butter, cut into pieces
1 cup coarsely chopped walnuts or pecans

Heat the oven to 350 degrees. Butter the baking tins, or line them with paper liners.

Make the cakes: Cream the butter until smooth in a mixer fitted with a paddle attachment (or using a hand mixer). With the mixer running, slowly add the sugar and mix. Add the eggs and mix until the mixture is light and fluffy.

Sift together the sifted flour, baking soda, baking powder, and salt. Working in batches, add the flour mixture to the butter–sugar mixture, alternating with dollops of sour cream. Mix in the cranberries. Pour or spoon the batter into the prepared cups, filling them no more than three-quarters full.

Make the topping: Combine the brown sugar, flour, and cinnamon in a medium bowl. Add the butter pieces and, using your fingertips, pinch the ingredients together into a sandy, crumbly mixture. Add the walnuts and mix. Sprinkle the mixture over the cakes.

Bake until the cakes are risen and browned, 20 to 25 minutes. Let them cool for 10 minutes in the pan.

tasting trio

Roasted Plums on the Half Shell with Fromage Blanc

Baby French Toast with Blueberry Stuffing

Cranberry–Walnut Cakes

frozen creamy dark chocolate sandwiches

MAKES 12 TO 16

If you are a fan of the Devil Dog, the Oreo cookie, and the ice cream sandwich, this dessert is for you. Dark chocolate, with its bitter edge, makes a wonderful contrast with the mild milkiness of whipped cream. To make them even more like childhood ice cream sandwiches, I always serve these individually wrapped in parchment paper: Unwrapping as you eat is part of the fun. Eventually, of course, you'll have to abandon the paper and devour the lusciously melting remains.

For color, you could wrap colored cellophane around the parchment, making a twist at each end. If you have a square platter or plates for serving, use them: The effect will be fabulous.

These can be made well in advance, wrapped, and kept frozen indefinitely.

you'll need

A large baking sheet with sides, about 13 x 17 inches, buttered and lined with parchment or wax paper

FOR THE CAKE

1¼ cups cake flour
½ cup cocoa powder, preferably Dutch-processed
1 teaspoon baking soda
½ teaspoon salt
8 tablespoons (1 stick) cool unsalted butter
1½ cups sugar
3 eggs
1 cup buttermilk (see page 13)
1 teaspoon pure vanilla extract

FOR THE FILLING

2 cups chilled heavy cream
2 tablespoons sugar
½ teaspoon pure vanilla extract

Make the cake: Heat the oven to 350 degrees.

Sift the flour, cocoa powder, baking soda, and salt together three times (this is to make the cake extra light).

Cream the butter in a mixer fitted with a whisk attachment until smooth and fluffy. Add the sugar and mix. One at a time, add the eggs, mixing after each addition. Beat until fluffy and light.

With the mixer running at low speed, add a third of the dry ingredients and mix. Add half of the buttermilk and mix. Add another third of the dry ingredients and mix. Add the remaining buttermilk and the vanilla and mix. Add the remaining dry ingredients and mix until smooth. Pour the batter into the pan and spread it out into the corners.

Bake until the cake is set in the center and springy, 20 to 25 minutes. Let it cool in the pan on a wire rack. Turn the cake out onto a work surface and peel off the paper. Flip the cake over again so the shiny top side is facing up. Cut the cake in half crosswise, so you have two rectangles of cake.

Make the filling: Whip the cream with the sugar and vanilla until stiff. Spread an even layer over one rectangle of cake, then flip the other rectangle over (so that the shiny side faces down, and will touch the cream) and place it on top of the cream. Freeze for 1 hour.

Cut the cake into bar-shaped sandwiches, about 2 × 3 inches each. Wrap them individually in parchment or wax paper, as you would wrap a present, and serve frozen.

(The recipe can be made several weeks in advance and kept frozen, in a plastic container or individually wrapped in plastic wrap.)

tasting trio

Vacherins with Raspberries and Cream

Orange Tuiles

Frozen Creamy Sandwiches

cannelés (slow-baked french vanilla cakes)

MAKES 16 TO 20

See photograph, page 152

There has never been a more peculiar cake, or a more peculiar recipe than the one for *cannelés*. You must taste them to love them—and you will.

After a trip to southwestern France, my friend Larry arrived in my kitchen with a dusty wooden box that looked as if it had been found in a cave. It was packed with six tiny grooved copper molds and a cake recipe written in French. As I followed it (slowly), I kept thinking "This can't be right!" The cannelés seemed to have too much sugar and too little flour, and they seemed to take much too long to make. But they were perfect, as Larry confirmed when I baked them for his next birthday.

As it turns out, cannelés are like tiny popovers, with a tender, eggy, vanilla-perfumed interior and a crust that is baked and baked and baked to a dark brown, wonderfully chewy rind. They are classics in southwestern France, where they make a perfect teatime snack with a *tisane* (herb tea) or hot chocolate.

Note that this recipe takes two days, but each step is utterly simple. While the batter is developing in your fridge, the vanilla flavor permeates the mixture and the batter becomes tender and smooth.

you'll need

12 to 16 *cannelé* molds or other baking molds (about 4 ounces each), or 2 muffin tins (see page 18)

3¼ cups milk
1 vanilla bean, split lengthwise
4 tablespoons unsalted butter
3 eggs
2 tablespoons dark rum
2 cups plus 2 tablespoons sugar
1½ cups all-purpose flour

Two days before you plan to serve the dessert, combine the milk and vanilla bean in a saucepan and bring to a boil. Immediately turn off the heat and let the milk cool to room temperature. Cover and refrigerate overnight to infuse the vanilla flavor into the milk.

The next day, melt the butter. Whisk the eggs into the chilled milk mixture, then whisk in the rum and butter. Add the sugar and flour and whisk to combine. Refrigerate overnight.

Heat the oven to 400 degrees. Thickly butter the baking molds and chill them until the butter is firm. Remove the vanilla bean from the batter and whisk the batter one more time to mix it thoroughly. Pour or ladle the batter into the molds, filling them not quite to the top (they will expand a bit as they bake).

Place the filled molds on a cookie sheet or in a shallow pan. Bake until the cannelés are very, very dark brown on the outside, about 1 hour. Check them regularly after the first 45 minutes to make sure they're dark brown but not turning black. When finished, they will be very dark brown caramelized and chewy on the outside, and tender and eggy on the inside. While they are still warm, turn the cannelés out of the molds.

tasting trio

Fannie's Banana–Blueberry–Sour Cream Salad

Orange–Honey-Glazed Almonds

Cannelés

saffron madeleines

MAKES ABOUT 50 SMALL, 25 LARGE

To me, madeleines are everything wonderful about French cuisine baked into a tiny butter cake. Eating warm madeleines out of a paper bag on a Paris park bench is my idea of a great vacation.

After much tinkering, this madeleine recipe has become my favorite. The additions to the basic batter may seem radical, but their effects are very subtle. The saffron ensures a beautiful golden color and adds a light, fragrant floweriness (although you can use less than the 2 tablespoons specified in the recipe, or leave it out altogether to show off the flavor of the honey). The honey and light brown sugar keep the finished cakes moist, and they combine with the browned butter to deepen the flavor. Using cake flour gives the madeleines just the right melting texture.

It's wonderful to serve these right out of the oven, resting on a pristine white folded napkin. In any case, serve them the same day you bake them.

you'll need

- 2 madeleine or mini-madeleine pans, or 2 mini-muffin tins (see page 18)
- A pastry bag (optional; see page 15) with a large plain tip
- A pastry brush

8 tablespoons unsalted butter, divided
At least 1 tablespoon saffron threads (2 tablespoons is best, but saffron is expensive)
4 eggs
½ cup plus 2 tablespoons granulated sugar
2 tablespoons light brown sugar
⅛ teaspoon salt
2½ teaspoons baking powder
1½ cups cake flour
¼ teaspoon pure vanilla extract
1 tablespoon honey

Make the saffron brown butter: Melt 6 tablespoons of the butter with the saffron in a heavy pan over medium heat. After it melts, continue to cook the butter, watching carefully. It will foam and subside, then separate into golden butterfat and cloudy white milk solids. The milk solids will begin to brown.

When they are lightly browned and the butter smells nutty and toasted, remove it from the heat and set it aside for 5 minutes to infuse. Strain through a fine strainer to remove the saffron threads and toasted milk solids.

Whip the eggs and sugars in a mixer fitted with a whisk attachment until light and fluffy. Mixing at low speed, add the dry ingredients. Add the vanilla extract, honey, and the saffron butter and mix to combine well. *(The recipe can be made up to this point and kept refrigerated for up to 3 days.)*

When ready to bake, melt the remaining 2 tablespoons of butter. Double-butter the baking pans: Use a pastry brush to thickly coat the pans with melted butter, then chill them in the freezer until firm. Repeat to make a thick coat of cold butter.

Heat the oven to 375 degrees. Pipe or spoon the batter into the madeleine molds, filling them no more than three-quarters full. *(The recipe can be made up to this point early in the day, then refrigerated until ready to bake. Add 1 minute to the baking time.)*

Bake until the madeleines are firm, 5 to 8 minutes for large madeleines and 5 minutes for miniatures. Immediately turn or knock them out of the pans and serve, or let them cool to room temperature, store them in an airtight container, and serve them later the same day.

tasting trio

Banana Brûlée Spoonfuls

Sesame Brittle

Saffron Madeleines

tangerine marmalade babycakes

MAKES ABOUT 45

This classic *petit-four* is all about a spectacular flavor combination: tangerine and almond. In each moist mouthful, sweet, tangy citrus cuts right through the round, rich flavor of nuts. Then there's a crackly surface of confectioners' sugar and a bright, jewellike bit of fresh tangerine on top.

Almond paste, available at baking supply stores, is slightly different from marzipan; the paste is darker and more coarsely ground than marzipan. But marzipan will work fine too.

you'll need

- About 45 miniature ribbed paper cupcake liners
- A cookie sheet
- A pastry bag, optional (see page 15) with a large plain tip

1 tangerine (or navel orange, if tangerines are unavailable)
13 ounces almond paste or marzipan
1 tablespoon tangerine or orange marmalade
3 eggs
1 egg yolk
Heaping ¼ cup all-purpose flour
7 tablespoons unsalted butter, melted
¼ cup confectioners' sugar

Grate the zest from the tangerine and set aside. Peel the tangerine and remove any white strings. Section it and cut each section into 4 pieces. Remove any pits.

Arrange the paper cups on a cookie sheet. Heat the oven to 350 degrees.

Combine the almond paste, marmalade, and tangerine zest in a mixer fitted with a paddle attachment and mix until smooth. One at a time, add the eggs and mix in. Add the yolk and the flour and mix in at low speed. Add the melted butter and mix. Transfer to a pastry bag.

Pipe the batter into the paper cups, filling each one three-quarters full. Place a quarter of a tangerine section cut side down on each teacake, then sprinkle them all liberally with confectioners' sugar, making sure the tops are lightly but completely covered (use a shaker or strainer if you like). Bake until the cakes are firm and lightly browned, 25 to 30 minutes. Cool the cakes and serve at room temperature, in the paper cups.

tasting trio

Chocolate Pots-de-Crème

Coconut Pistachio Tuiles

Tangerine Marmalade Babycakes

very red velvet cupcakes

MAKES
12

See photograph, page 148

There's nothing like a lavishly frosted cupcake to bring back the best childhood memories. Remember when something to eat could make you so happy? I still get a little thrill of anticipation from peeling off the ribbed paper cup.

This cupcake also offers some grown-up pleasures. I love the scandalous, vampy red of red velvet cake, and it's fun to conceal it with an innocent top of pure white frosting. This frosting is particularly stiff and white (and it will stay that way at room temperature), but you can use any white frosting. Use white paper cups and the sides will look like a pretty pale pink. You can make them any size you like, but make sure not to fill the cups more than three-quarters full. And don't skimp on the food coloring!

you'll need

- A muffin tin (see page 18)
- 12 white ribbed paper cupcake liners
- A small icing spatula

FOR THE BATTER

- 1 cup vegetable shortening
- 2 eggs
- 1½ cups sugar
- 2 tablespoons cocoa powder
- 2 ounces red food coloring (2 small bottles)
- 2½ cups cake flour
- 1 teaspoon salt
- 1 teaspoon baking soda
- 1 cup buttermilk (see page 13)
- 1 teaspoon pure vanilla extract
- 1 teaspoon red- or white-wine vinegar

FOR THE FROSTING

- 1 cup milk
- 2 tablespoons all-purpose flour
- 16 tablespoons (2 sticks) cool unsalted butter
- 1 cup confectioners' sugar
- 1 teaspoon pure vanilla extract

Make the cupcakes: Line the muffin tin with cupcake liners. Heat the oven to 350 degrees.

Cream the shortening, eggs, and sugar together in a mixer fitted with a paddle attachment until smooth and fluffy.

Whisk the cocoa powder and food coloring into a smooth paste in a small bowl. Add the paste to the shortening mixture and mix.

Sift the flour, salt, and baking soda together. Combine the buttermilk, vanilla, and vinegar in a bowl. With the mixer running at low speed, add about a third of the dry ingredients to the shortening mixture and mix. Then add about half of the wet ingredients and mix. Add another third of the dry ingredients and mix. Add the remaining wet ingredients and mix. Add the remaining dry ingredients and mix until smooth.

Pour or ladle the batter into the cupcake papers, filling them three-quarters full. Bake until the cupcakes are firm to the touch in the center, 15 to 20 minutes. Let them cool in the pan.

Meanwhile, make the frosting: Put the milk in a saucepan and whisk in the flour. Bring to a simmer over medium heat and simmer until thickened, about 5 minutes, whisking often. Cover and let cool to room temperature.

Cream the butter, sugar, and vanilla in a mixer fitted with a paddle attachment until light and very fluffy. Add the cooled thickened milk and mix until smooth. When the cupcakes are cool, use the icing spatula to frost the tops.

tasting trio

Root Beer Slush in Vanilla Cream Cordial Cups

Peanut Butterballs

Very Red Velvet Cupcakes

pound cake tea sandwiches

MAKES ABOUT 24

A platter of these finger-size sandwiches, festively striped with yellow cake, pink filling, and dark chocolate, is an instant tea party. Kids and grown-ups love them equally, and they are outrageously easy to make.

You bake a simple pound cake to serve as the bread, then paint each slice with melted chocolate. The cooled chocolate forms a hard (and delicious) waterproof layer that keeps the creamy raspberry filling from making the "bread" soggy. Each component of the sandwich remains separate and fresh.

To show off the stripes, turn the cut sandwiches on their sides and arrange them in a flat basket lined with a tea towel.

you'll need

A 6-cup loaf pan, greased and lined with parchment or wax paper

FOR THE CAKE

4 eggs
10 tablespoons unsalted butter, melted, or ⅔ cup vegetable oil
1⅓ cups sugar
1 teaspoon pure vanilla extract
2 cups all-purpose flour
2 teaspoons baking powder
⅔ cup whole, 2% fat, or 1% fat milk

4 ounces semisweet chocolate, melted (see page 11)

FOR THE FILLINGS

8 ounces cream cheese, warmed slightly in the microwave or at room temperature
1 tablespoon honey
½ cup raspberries

Make the cake: Heat the oven to 350 degrees.

Beat the eggs in a mixer fitted with a whisk attachment until fluffy and light. With the mixer running, drizzle in the butter or oil. Add the sugar and mix. Add the vanilla extract and mix. Combine the flour and baking powder. With the mixer running at low speed, add about a third of the dry ingredients to the egg mixture and mix. Then add half the milk and mix. Add another third of the dry ingredients and mix. Add the remaining milk and mix. Add the remaining dry ingredients and mix until smooth. Pour the batter into the pan and bake until the cake springs back in the center when touched, about 40 minutes. Let the cake cool in the pan on a wire rack.

Use a serrated knife to cut the cake into ½-inch-thick slices. Spread one face of each slice of cake with melted chocolate; this is to coat and waterproof the cake. Place in the refrigerator to set while you make the filling.

In a food processor, blend the cream cheese, honey, and raspberries until smooth and spreadable. Spread the cream cheese mixture over the chocolate on half of the cake slices. Top each one with another slice of cake, chocolate side down. Use a serrated knife to cut the brown crusts off the sandwiches and then cut each sandwich into three 1-inch-wide "fingers." Turn the sandwiches on their sides to show off the stripes, and serve.

tasting trio

Pineapple and Melon Ball Brochettes

Mint–Chocolate-Chip Meringues

Pound Cake Tea Sandwiches

sour cream seed cakes with earl grey glaze

MAKES 8 MINI-LOAVES OR 12 CAKES

Although my mother's family left Hungary a generation before she was born, she still told me some of the old stories—like the one about a grandmother who made a batch of seed cakes for her grandson. A goose stole the cakes as they were cooling, making her so angry that she killed the goose and made him into a featherbed for her grandson!

Poppy seeds figured prominently in my mother's and my grandmother's baking, as did the sour cream that gives this cake batter its wonderful tang. My addition is the use of Earl Grey tea as the liquid in the batter and in the glaze; its subtle scent (from bergamot, a citrus oil) perfumes the cakes beautifully.

you'll need

8 mini-loaf pans (2 x 3½ inches) or a muffin tin, buttered and floured (unless your pans are nonstick)

FOR THE CAKE

¼ cup poppy seeds
2 tablespoons fennel seeds
½ cup strong, freshly brewed Earl Grey tea
2 cups all-purpose flour
1 teaspoon baking soda
1½ teaspoons baking powder
¼ teaspoon salt
8 tablespoons (1 stick) cool unsalted butter
1 cup sugar
2 eggs
1½ teaspoons pure vanilla extract
1 cup sour cream

FOR THE GLAZE

¼ cup strong, freshly brewed Earl Grey tea
1½ cups confectioners' sugar

Make the cake: Combine both kinds of seeds and the ½ cup tea in a bowl. Let the seeds soak to absorb and soften while you prepare the other ingredients.

Heat the oven to 350 degrees.

Sift together the flour, baking soda, baking powder, and salt and set aside. Cream the butter until smooth in a mixer fitted with a whisk attachment (or using a hand mixer). Add the sugar and cream together until soft and fluffy. One at a time, add the eggs, mixing well after each addition. Add the vanilla and mix.

With the mixer on low speed, add a third of the dry ingredients and mix. Then add half of the sour cream and mix. Add another third of the dry ingredients and mix. Add the remaining sour cream and mix. Add the remaining dry ingredients and mix until smooth. Add the seeds with their soaking liquid and mix until smooth.

Pour into the pans and bake until the cakes are firm in the center, 25 to 30 minutes. Let them cool in the pans.

Meanwhile, make the glaze: Whisk the ¼ cup of tea and the confectioners' sugar in a bowl until smooth.

When the cakes have cooled, turn them out onto a work surface. Give the glaze a stir. Dip the bottom (the narrower side) of each cake lightly into the glaze until coated. Turn over so the glazed side becomes the top and set the cakes aside to let the glaze soak in and harden.

tasting trio

Vanilla Snow with Maple Syrup

Green Grapes Glacé

Sour Cream Seed Cakes with Earl Grey Glaze

Orange–Vanilla "Fried Eggs" on Cinnamon Toast

Lemon Cream Daisies

Tea Sandwiches with Vanilla Custard and Rose Petals

Brittle-Topped Vanilla–Butterscotch Pudding Parfaits

Baby French Toast with Creamy Blueberry Stuffing

Double-Vanilla Crème Brûlées ◎ Banana Brûlée Spoonfuls

Cinnamon–Basmati Rice Pudding

Toasted Coconut Risotto with Pecans

Cherry Charlottes

Bread Puddings with Orange Marmalade

creamy BITES

orange–vanilla "fried eggs" on cinnamon toast

MAKES 6 TO 8

I've been making these for years, and I still giggle every time I see one. The fried eggs are put together from a *panna cotta* "white" and an orange gelatin "yolk," and they look just like the original! Panna cotta is a simple Italian dessert of cream (or milk) just set with gelatin, slightly wobbly and very soothing. The orange and cream taste wonderful together. Cinnamon toast, always one of my favorite breakfasts, is a delicious and, of course, appropriate pairing.

you'll need

- A shallow pan, about 11 x 17 inches
- A shallow pan, about 9 x 13 inches
- A round cookie cutter, about 2½ inches across
- A round cookie cutter, about 1 inch across

FOR THE WHITES

- 1¾ cups whole milk
- ½ vanilla bean, split lengthwise
- ¾ cup sugar
- 2 tablespoons cold water
- 1 tablespoon powdered gelatin
- 1¾ cups heavy cream, whipped to soft peaks (not stiff)

FOR THE YOLKS

- 1⅓ cups orange juice
- 1 tablespoon powdered gelatin

FOR SERVING (OPTIONAL)

- Good-quality white bread or brioche, 1 slice per serving
- Butter
- Cinnamon sugar

Make the whites: Combine the milk, vanilla bean, and sugar in a saucepan. Heat just to a boil, then immediately turn off the heat and set aside for 10 minutes to infuse the vanilla flavor.

Meanwhile, pour the cold water into a bowl, sprinkle the gelatin over the surface, and set aside for 5 minutes. Add the gelatin mixture to the hot milk mixture and stir to dissolve the gelatin. Fill a large bowl with ice and cover with cold water. Strain the hot milk mixture into a smaller, preferably metal bowl and rest it in the ice bath to cool. Stir often, scraping the sides with a rubber spatula. The mixture will thicken as it cools. When the mixture is just starting to set, fold in the whipped cream. Pour the mixture into the larger (11 × 17-inch) pan. The mixture should be about ¼ inch thick in the pan. Chill it uncovered until it is completely set, about 2 hours.

Meanwhile, make the yolks: Pour the orange juice into a bowl, sprinkle the gelatin over the surface, and set aside for 5 minutes. Heat in the microwave for 30 seconds (or on the stove), stirring to dissolve the gelatin. Pour the mixture into the smaller (9 × 13-inch) pan. The mixture should be about ¼ inch thick in the pan. Chill it uncovered until it is completely set, about 2 hours.

When ready to serve, cut the crusts off the bread and toast it. Butter the toast and sprinkle it with cinnamon sugar. Using round cookie cutters, cut large rounds of the "white" mixture. Cut small rounds of the "yolk" mixture.

Put a piece of cinnamon toast on each serving plate. Using a spatula to lift the "whites," place one on each piece of toast. Place a "yolk" on top and serve immediately.

tasting trio

Devil's Peaks with Double-Chocolate Drizzle

Sesame Brittle

Orange–Vanilla "Fried Eggs" on Cinnamon Toast

lemon cream daisies

MAKES ABOUT 40

See photograph, page 154

It's amazing how often, when I'm planning a dinner menu, the perfect dessert is clearly a lemon tart. Rich but always refreshing, a good lemon tart is simply elegant and cheery, and it can harmonize with so many other flavors.

Although these are miniature tarts, they're actually easier than usual: They are made with store-bought puff pastry. I love the contrast of flaky-crisp pastry layers and deep, plush custard. If you don't have a flower-shaped or fluted cookie cutter, feel free to use plain rounds. Just make sure to gently cut and lift out the center to make room for the lemon cream.

you'll need

- A fluted cookie cutter, 2 to 2½ inches across
- A round cookie cutter, 1 inch across
- A cookie sheet, ungreased

2 eggs
½ cup sugar
⅓ cup freshly squeezed lemon juice (from 3 to 4 lemons)
Freshly grated zest of ½ lemon
2 tablespoons unsalted butter, slightly softened at room temperature
½ cup chilled heavy cream
1 package of puff pastry (2 sheets), thawed
2 tablespoons chopped pistachios

Bring about 2 inches of water to a simmer in a large saucepan. In a mixer fitted with a whisk attachment (or using a hand mixer), whip the eggs and sugar together until very light yellow and fluffy. Mix in the lemon juice and lemon zest. Rest the mixing bowl in the saucepan, with the bowl's base resting above—not in—the simmering water (pour out some water if necessary). Cook, whisking occasionally, until the mixture is thickened and custardy, about 10 minutes.

Meanwhile, half-fill a large bowl with ice and cover with cold water.

Remove the bowl with the lemon curd in it from the hot water and whisk in the butter until melted. Rest the bottom of the bowl in the ice bath and let the lemon curd cool, folding the mixture occasionally to cool and thicken it.

In a mixer fitted with a whisk attachment (or using a hand mixer), whip the cream until stiff. Fold it into the cooled lemon curd. Cover and refrigerate the lemon cream until ready to serve. *(The recipe can be made up to this point and kept refrigerated for up to 3 days.)*

Heat the oven to 350 degrees. Flour a work surface and lay out the puff pastry. Roll the sheets lightly with a rolling pin until smooth and flattened. Use the large cookie cutter to cut out rounds from the puff pastry. Then use the small, round cutter to push halfway down in the center of each round. Do not pull out the centers; you'll hollow them out after they are baked. Arrange the rounds on the cookie sheet and bake until golden brown, 15 to 20 minutes. After 10 minutes, rotate the pan to ensure even cooking. When the rounds are baked, immediately remove them to a wire rack and let them cool to room temperature.

Cut around the centers with a paring knife to loosen, but don't cut all the way through to the bottom. You want to leave a thin layer of pastry to hold the filling. Hollow out the centers to make a depression in the center of each pastry round. Or, just push the pastry down in the center with your thumb.

Not more than 4 hours before serving, spoon or pipe a generous dollop of lemon cream into each pastry round. Sprinkle with chopped pistachios. Serve within 4 hours.

tasting trio

Nutmeg Ice Cream with Gingerbread Wafers

Green Grapes Glacé

Lemon Cream Daisies

tea sandwiches with vanilla custard and rose petals

MAKES ABOUT 36

As a working chef and the mother of a five-year-old, my favorite fantasy involves a long, lazy summer tea party in the garden with my girlfriends, all of us wearing hats and magically liberated for the entire afternoon (and my garden magically transformed into a walled English garden with herbaceous borders). This recipe deliciously evokes that spirit, though the reality eludes me so far!

A classic French napoleon, one of my favorite desserts, layers buttery pastry and vanilla custard; this sandwich brings those elements together in a simpler way. The rose petals are more for color and mood than flavor; use any deep-colored rose so that the petals will be visible against the pale background. They are perfectly edible; just rinse them well and dry them on paper towels.

These sandwiches are ideal for a bridal or baby shower, or any garden party. Serve them on antique tea towels.

you'll need

- A cookie sheet, ungreased
- A small offset spatula or a sandwich spreader

FOR THE BRIOCHE

1½ cups all-purpose flour
1¼ cups plus 2 tablespoons bread flour
1 teaspoon salt
¼ cup sugar
1 ounce fresh yeast or 2 (¼-ounce) envelopes of active dry yeast
2 tablespoons warm water
4 eggs
8 ounces (2 sticks) cold unsalted butter, cut into pieces

FOR THE FILLINGS

3 roses, any color (but not too pale)
2 cups whole, 2% fat, or 1% fat milk

½ vanilla bean, split lengthwise
6 egg yolks
⅔ cup sugar
¼ cup cornstarch
1 tablespoon cold unsalted butter

Make the brioche: At least one day before you plan to serve the dessert, combine the flours, salt, and 2 tablespoons of the sugar in a mixer fitted with a dough hook, and mix. Dissolve the yeast in the warm water. With the mixer running at low speed, add the yeast mixture and eggs to the flour mixture and mix well until incorporated. Add the butter and mix at medium speed until smooth, about 10 minutes. Do not skimp on the mixing time; this is how the dough gets kneaded. Cover the bowl tightly with plastic wrap, and refrigerate overnight.

The next day, turn the dough out onto a floured work surface. Flour the rolling pin and roll the dough into a 9 × 13-inch rectangle, about ½ inch thick. Transfer to the cookie sheet. Loosely drape plastic wrap over the dough and let the dough rise in a warm place until doubled in bulk, 1 to 2 hours.

Preheat the oven to 350 degrees. Remove the plastic wrap from the dough and sprinkle with the remaining 2 tablespoons of sugar. Bake until the brioche is golden brown, 15 to 20 minutes. After 10 minutes, rotate the pan to ensure even cooking. When the brioche is baked, immediately remove it to a wire rack and let it cool to room temperature.

Meanwhile, make the fillings: Separate the rose petals and swish them around in a bowl of water. Rinse and set them aside to dry on paper towels, or spin them dry in a salad spinner. Refrigerate.

recipe continues on next page

Combine the milk and vanilla bean in a small saucepan and bring just to a boil over medium heat. Immediately turn off the heat and set the milk aside to infuse for 10 minutes.

Whisk the egg yolks and sugar together until light and fluffy. Add the cornstarch and whisk vigorously until no lumps remain. Whisk in ¼ cup of the hot milk mixture until incorporated. Whisk in the remaining hot milk mixture, reserving the empty saucepan.

Pour the mixture through a strainer back into the saucepan. Cook over medium-high heat, whisking constantly, until the mixture is thickened and slowly boiling. Remove the pan from the heat and stir in the butter. Let the custard cool slightly. Cover it with plastic wrap, lightly pressing the plastic against the surface to prevent a skin from forming. Chill for at least 2 hours or until ready to serve. *(The custard can be made up to 2 days in advance and kept refrigerated.)*

Not more than 2 hours before serving, use a serrated knife to slice the sheet of brioche horizontally in half. Spread the bottom and top (the cut sides) generously with the custard. Sprinkle the rose petals over the bottom, covering the surface entirely. Place the top brioche on and press lightly. Using a heavy, large serrated knife, cut into finger sandwiches, discarding the edges. The sandwiches can be bar-shaped (about 1 × 2½ inches) or square (about 2 × 2 inches). Serve within 2 hours.

tasting trio

Orange Tuiles

Ruby Raspberry Jellies

Tea Sandwiches with Vanilla Custard and Rose Petals

brittle-topped vanilla–butterscotch pudding parfaits

MAKES 10 TO 15

You know those striped pudding cups your kids beg you to buy—the ones you've been sneaking out of the fridge after their bedtime? Here's how to make them with no additives, no stabilizers, and plenty of glorious fresh flavor and rich texture. Real vanilla bean and an easy homemade butterscotch make these puddings taste truly wonderful, and then the crunch of nut brittle on top pushes the dessert right over the edge into heavenly.

Both vanilla and butterscotch pudding start with a vanilla base, so you make a large batch and then split it to make two different flavors.

you'll need

- 2 pastry bags fitted with large plain tips, or 2 thick, resealable plastic bags (see page 15)
- 10 to 15 decorative shot glasses, cordial cups, demitasse cups, or other small glasses

- 2¼ cups whole milk
- 1 cup heavy cream
- 1 vanilla bean, split lengthwise
- 3 tablespoons unsalted butter
- ½ cup plus 2 tablespoons (packed) light brown sugar
- 2 egg yolks
- ¼ cup cornstarch
- ¼ teaspoon salt
- 6 tablespoons granulated sugar
- ⅓ cup chopped Cinnamon Peanut Brittle, optional (page 183)

Combine the milk, cream, and vanilla bean in a large saucepan and bring to a simmer over medium-high heat. Immediately turn off the heat and set the mixture aside for 10 minutes to infuse. Remove the vanilla bean. Pour half of the mixture into another saucepan and set aside for the vanilla pudding.

recipe continues on next page

Make the butterscotch pudding: In a medium, heavy skillet, melt the butter over medium heat. Stir in the brown sugar, raise the heat to medium-high, and cook for 3 to 5 minutes, stirring constantly, to caramelize the mixture. (You'll smell a characteristic nutty caramel scent when the butter browns, signaling that the mixture is ready.)

Whisking constantly, slowly add the butter–brown sugar mixture to one pan of hot milk–cream mixture. If the butterscotch isn't smooth, blend it for 20 seconds with a hand blender or pour it through a fine sieve.

Put one of the egg yolks in a medium bowl. Whisk in about ½ cup of the butterscotch mixture. Whisk in 2 tablespoons of the cornstarch and ⅛ teaspoon of the salt until dissolved. Whisk the cornstarch mixture back into the butterscotch saucepan.

Cook over medium-high heat, whisking constantly, until the mixture is thickened and just boiling. When the whisk leaves trail marks on the bottom of the pot and a few large bubbles boil up to the top, the pudding is sufficiently thickened. Let it cool slightly and transfer it to a pastry bag or thick, resealable plastic bag.

Make the vanilla pudding: Whisk the granulated sugar into the remaining egg yolk in a medium bowl. Then add ½ cup of the reserved vanilla–hot milk mixture and whisk well. Add the remaining 2 tablespoons of cornstarch and the remaining ⅛ teaspoon of salt and mix, then add the rest of the vanilla–hot milk mixture.

Return the mixture to a saucepan and cook over medium-high heat, whisking constantly, until it is thickened and just boiling. When the whisk leaves trail marks on the bottom of the pot and a few large bubbles boil up to the top, the pudding is sufficiently thickened. Let it cool slightly and transfer it to a pastry bag or thick, resealable plastic bag.

If using plastic bags, snip one corner off of each one. Pipe striped layers of the puddings into the serving cups and chill, covered, for at least 2 hours or overnight. Serve the parfaits chilled, with chopped brittle on top.

tasting trio

Chocolate–Mint Tiddlywinks

Animal Crackers

Brittle-Topped Vanilla–Butterscotch Pudding Parfaits

baby french toast with creamy blueberry stuffing

MAKES 16

French toast for dessert may sound odd, but look at the ingredients: It's almost identical to bread pudding! This recipe falls somewhere between the two, making it ideal for a special breakfast or comforting dessert.

To make these miniature stacks, you'll simply quarter slices of good bread into little squares. A slight enrichment of the usual French toast soak—I add half-and-half and an extra egg yolk—makes the squares puffy and soft, and will help them brown even more deeply than usual. Finally, instead of butter and syrup, serve with a zingy maple, orange, and blueberry cream.

8 slices store-bought brioche (try a French bakery), challah, or soft white bread
1 egg plus 1 egg yolk
Pinch of salt
¼ cup sugar
¼ teaspoon pure vanilla extract
½ cup half-and-half
½ cup milk
2 tablespoons unsalted butter
1 cup blueberries, fresh or frozen
1 tablespoon maple syrup or brown sugar
1 tablespoon orange marmalade
½ cup sour cream or yogurt

Cut the crusts off the bread slices and cut each slice into quarters to make squares, about 1½ inches on each side.

Whisk the egg and yolk in a medium bowl. Whisk in the salt, sugar, and vanilla. Gradually whisk in the half-and-half and the milk. Pour the mixture into a shallow baking dish. Working in batches if necessary, place the bread pieces in the egg mixture and let them soak, then turn them and soak on the other side.

Melt the butter in a skillet until it is foamy and very hot. Working in batches, brown the soaked bread on both sides.

Meanwhile, gently fold the blueberries, maple syrup, marmalade, and sour cream together in a bowl.

To serve, arrange half of the browned bread squares on a platter, and top each with a spoonful of the blueberry stuffing. Top off with another piece of bread and another small dollop of blueberry stuffing. Serve immediately.

tasting trio

Coffee Suckers on Cinnamon Sticks

Taffy Lady Apples

Baby French Toast with Creamy Blueberry Stuffing

double-vanilla crème brûlées

MAKES 12 TO 20 SMALL SERVINGS

Very rich, very smooth, very thick: This recipe offers a pure vanilla hit, with no other flavors to distract from its creamy sweetness. Vanilla beans, like wine grapes, have distinct flavors depending on how and where they are grown. Vanilla extract is like table wine, a homogenized mixture of styles that can be excellent; but a vanilla bean, like a single-grape wine (think Pinot Noir or Cabernet), will always have more character. This recipe uses both.

The burnt-sugar coating on top of crème brûlée can be substantial and thick, or shatteringly thin—it's a matter of personal preference.

you'll need

12 to 20 miniature ramekins or gratin dishes (see page 19)

A hot-water bath (see page 21)

A kitchen torch (optional)

2⅓ cups heavy cream
⅓ cup half-and-half
½ vanilla bean, split lengthwise
8 egg yolks
½ cup granulated sugar
¼ teaspoon pure vanilla extract
½ cup coarse sugar, raw sugar, or demerara sugar

Heat the oven to 300 degrees.

Heat the cream, half-and-half, and vanilla bean in a saucepan over medium heat just until it comes to a boil. Immediately turn off the heat. Set the mixture aside to infuse for 10 minutes.

Whisk the egg yolks with the sugar in a large bowl just until combined. Whisking constantly, gradually pour in the hot cream mixture, then add the vanilla extract. Strain the mixture into a pitcher to smooth it and to remove the vanilla bean.

Divide the custard among the ramekins. Arrange them in the hot-water bath; the water may be very shallow, but that's fine. Bake in the center of the oven until the custards are set, 30 to 35 minutes. Remove from the water bath and let cool for 15 minutes. Tightly cover each custard with plastic wrap, making sure the plastic does not touch the surface. Refrigerate for at least 2 hours. *(The recipe can be made up to this point and kept refrigerated for up to 3 days.)*

When ready to serve, preheat a broiler to very hot (or fire up your kitchen torch). Sprinkle the surface of each custard with an even layer of coarse sugar and place the ramekins on a baking sheet. Broil or torch the surface until the sugar is melted and well browned, about 1 minute. Let the crème brûlées cool slightly and serve immediately.

tasting trio

Crunchy Chocolate Haystacks

Vacherins with Raspberries and Cream

Double-Vanilla Crème Brûlées

banana brûlée spoonfuls

MAKES 20 TO 30 SPOONS

See photographs, page 155

For this creamy, crackly mouthful, the spoon itself is the serving dish. A simple vanilla custard fills the spoon, and the custard is topped with a slice of banana and a sprinkling of coarse sugar. Melt the top and you have a cold-hot-crisp-creamy bite of heaven, located somewhere between crème brûlée and banana cream pie.

I like the elegance of long-handled iced-tea spoons for this recipe, but any pretty spoons will do. Silver or stainless steel will work fine. To serve, arrange the spoons in rows on a rectangular platter, or in a spoke pattern on a round platter.

you'll need

- A 9-inch square baking dish, preferably not aluminum
- A hot-water bath (see page 21)
- 20 to 30 spoons, preferably long-handled (see above)
- A kitchen torch (optional)

1 cup heavy cream
⅓ cup half-and-half
¼ vanilla bean, split lengthwise, or ⅛ teaspoon pure vanilla extract
4 egg yolks
¼ cup granulated sugar
1 banana
¼ cup coarse sugar, raw sugar, or demerara sugar

Preheat the oven to 300 degrees.

Heat the cream, half-and-half, and vanilla bean in a medium saucepan over medium heat just to a boil. Immediately turn off the heat. Set aside to infuse for 10 minutes.

Whisk the egg yolks with the sugar in a large bowl just until combined. Whisking constantly, gradually pour in the hot cream mixture. Strain the mixture into the baking pan to smooth it and to remove the vanilla bean.

Place the pan in the hot-water bath. Bake in the center of the oven until the custard is set but not too firm (it will cook a little more as it cools), 40 to 50 minutes. Remove from the water bath and let cool for 15 minutes. Tightly cover the custard with plastic wrap, making sure the plastic does not touch the surface. *(The recipe can be made up to this point and kept refrigerated for up to 3 days.)*

Up to 4 hours before serving, fill the spoons with the chilled cooked custard by scooping each spoon into the pan of custard. Round the tops with a small spatula or a butter knife. Keep cold.

Right before serving, thinly slice the banana (about ⅛-inch thick). Heat a broiler to very hot (or fire up your kitchen torch). Top each spoonful of custard with a slice of banana, lightly pressing it onto the custard. Sprinkle the entire surface with a layer of coarse sugar and place each spoon on a baking sheet. Broil or torch the spoons until the sugar is melted and well browned, about 1 minute. Let the spoonfuls cool for 1 minute before serving.

tasting trio

Apricot Tartes Tatin

Florentines

Banana Brûlée Spoonfuls

cinnamon–basmati rice pudding

MAKES 12 SMALL SERVINGS

Everyone knows that rice pudding is a traditional old dessert, but whose tradition is it? Latin *arroz con leche,* Indian *chaaval ki kheer,* Jewish *reiz kugel,* and even French *riz au lait* are loved around the world. There are as many variations as there are countries, but rice and milk are the basics. After that, it's a free-for-all! I like a light, fluffy pudding like this one, that shows off the rice. Whipped cream lifts the texture up, and a bit of gelatin sets it there. Basmati rice, especially when rinsed, is extremely low in starch; it keeps the pudding from becoming stodgy.

you'll need

An ice-water bath (see page 21)

About 12 small serving cups or teacups

FOR THE RICE

½ cup basmati rice, rinsed
½ cup whole milk
½ cup cold water
Pinch of salt

FOR THE CUSTARD

2 teaspoons powdered gelatin
2 tablespoons cold water
1½ cups whole milk
½ teaspoon cinnamon
½ vanilla bean, split lengthwise
4 egg yolks
⅜ cup sugar
½ cup heavy cream, whipped

Make the rice: Bring the ingredients to a boil in a small, heavy saucepan. Reduce the heat to very low and cover tightly with a lid or foil. Cook without stirring until all the moisture is absorbed, 15 to 18 minutes. Turn off the heat and let the rice sit, covered, for at least 5 minutes or until you are ready to proceed.

Make the custard: Sprinkle the gelatin over the cold water and set the mixture aside to dissolve.

Combine the milk, cinnamon, and vanilla bean in a medium saucepan and bring just to a boil over medium heat. Immediately turn off the heat and let the milk sit for 10 minutes to infuse. Whisk the egg yolks and sugar together in a medium bowl, then gradually add the hot milk to the egg yolks in batches, whisking after each addition. Return the mixture to the saucepan and cook over low heat until the custard is thick enough to coat the back of a spoon. Turn off the heat.

Immediately stir the gelatin into the hot custard. Strain the mixture into a medium bowl and stir in the rice. Rest the bottom of the bowl in the ice bath and let the mixture cool, stirring frequently and scraping the sides of the bowl with a rubber spatula. As the mixture starts to thicken, about 10 minutes after you place it over the ice water, fold in the whipped cream (you don't want the gelatin mixture to set before you have a chance to fold in the cream, so check it frequently).

Immediately spoon the pudding into the serving dishes or teacups. Chill, covered, until ready to serve. *(The recipe can be made up to this point and kept refrigerated for up to 2 days.)*

tasting trio

White-Pepper Shortbread Cups

Orange–Cardamom Chocolate Truffles

Cinnamon–Basmati Rice Pudding

toasted coconut risotto with pecans

MAKES 12 SMALL SERVINGS

This dense, creamy risotto studded with nuts and orange zest is not your usual rice pudding! The recipe borrows from a traditional Italian risotto: from the short-grain, starchy Arborio rice I use, to the method of browning the aromatics (pecans, in this case) and rice in butter together as a first step. Toasted coconut adds a warm caramel undertone to the flavors. The finished product is thick and fragrant, but slightly loose, like rice bound in a creamy sauce. Crunchy bits of pecan make it perfect.

1 cup sweetened flaked coconut
1 tablespoon unsalted butter
¼ cup chopped pecans
1 cup Arborio rice, well rinsed in cold water
1¾ cups whole, 2% fat, or 1% fat milk
Freshly grated zest of ½ orange
2 tablespoons sugar
1 teaspoon pure vanilla extract
¾ cup heavy cream, chilled

you'll need

An ice-water bath (see page 21)

About 12 small serving cups or teacups

Heat the oven to 375 degrees. Spread the coconut out on a baking sheet and toast, stirring occasionally, until golden brown, about 10 minutes. Set aside to cool.

Melt the butter in a medium-size heavy saucepan. Add the pecans and sauté until lightly browned. Add the rinsed rice and stir to coat. Add 1 cup water, cover, and simmer the rice over very low heat without stirring until the liquid is absorbed. Add the milk, cover, and continue cooking without stirring until the rice is tender and the liquid is absorbed, about 25 minutes total.

Remove the mixture from the heat and stir in the coconut, orange zest, sugar, and vanilla extract. Rest the bottom of the pot in the ice bath and let the mixture cool, stirring often. Meanwhile, whip the cream. When the mixture is cool, fold in the whipped cream and spoon the pudding into the serving dishes. Chill, covered, until ready to serve. *(The recipe can be made up to this point and kept refrigerated for up to 2 days.)*

tasting trio

Raisin–Anise Biscotti

Chocolate Soufflé Pots

Toasted Coconut Risotto with Pecans

cherry charlottes

MAKES 8

Wisconsin cherries are just the kind of perfect ingredient that makes it fun to be a cook. They also make me glad to live in Chicago, where my son, Gio, and I can jump in the car, drive a couple of hours north, and eat ourselves silly when cherries come into season each June. Sour cherries, like cranberries, are especially wonderful in baking, with their combination of sour tang and sweet fruit.

Charlottes combine cake, cream, and fruit in a simple but luscious way. What makes a dessert a charlotte is the process of lining the pan with an absorbent layer of cake or, in this case, buttery bread. Charlotte pans are shaped like fez hats, wider at the top than the base; miniature ones are available from Williams-Sonoma (see Sources, page 300). But any ramekin will do. You may find it odd to put ramekins lined with plastic wrap into a hot oven, but the low temperature and the water bath keep the plastic from melting or burning.

you'll need

8 small charlotte molds (see above) or ramekins (see page 19)

A hot-water bath (see page 21)

- 2 cups half-and-half
- 2 cups heavy cream
- ⅛ teaspoon salt
- ½ vanilla bean, split lengthwise
- 6 eggs
- 1 cup sugar
- 1 loaf brioche (try a French bakery), or good-quality white bread
- ½ cup sour cherries, fresh, canned, or frozen, pitted and left whole
- Ice cream, for serving (optional)

Heat the half-and-half, cream, salt, and vanilla bean in a saucepan over medium heat, stirring occasionally to make sure the mixture doesn't burn or stick to the bottom of the pan. When the cream mixture reaches a fast simmer (do not let it boil), turn off the heat. Set the mixture aside to infuse for 10 minutes.

Whisk the eggs and sugar together in a large mixing bowl. Whisking constantly, gradually add the hot cream mixture. Strain into a large bowl to smooth the mixture and remove the vanilla bean. Let it cool slightly.

Cut off a few inches of the brioche loaf, remove the crusts, and cut the bread into small (½-inch) cubes to make ½ cup. Add the cubed brioche and the cherries to the custard and let soak for 30 minutes.

Meanwhile, line the molds with plastic wrap by buttering them first, then fitting the wrap inside. Slice the remaining bread into thin slices, cutting out rounds to fit the bottoms of the molds and vertical strips to neatly line the sides. Line the molds with the slices. Spoon the brioche and cherry mixture into the lined molds. Top off the molds with more custard, filling as much as possible. (There may be custard left over; reserve it, refrigerated.) Cover the molds with plastic wrap and refrigerate overnight.

When ready to bake, heat the oven to 300 degrees and prepare the hot-water bath. Uncover the molds. If there's room in the molds, top them off again with the remaining custard. Place the molds in the water bath and bake until the centers are set, about 1 hour.

Turn the charlottes out onto small plates and serve warm, with ice cream if desired. *(Or, let them cool and refrigerate them, covered, for up to 2 days. To serve, unmold onto individual serving plates—leave the plastic on—and microwave each charlotte for about 1 minute. Remove the plastic.)*

tasting trio

Tangerine Marmalade Babycakes

Crunchy Chocolate Haystacks

Cherry Charlottes

bread puddings with orange marmalade

MAKES 8

When I'm looking for a more elegant dessert than my usual chunky bread pudding, this individual version goes on the dessert menu immediately. Cutting the bread into rounds that fit neatly in your ramekins makes the dish much prettier; adding a layer of bittersweet orange marmalade means that each spoonful taps a warm vein of citrus flavor, a wonderful contrast to the creamy custard. This is a richer, more delicate, less "bready" bread pudding than most; feel free to leave out the marmalade, or use another flavor of jam.

you'll need

- 8 ramekins (see page 19)
- A cookie or biscuit cutter, the same diameter as your ramekins
- A hot-water bath (see page 21)

1 recipe brioche (from Tea Sandwiches with Vanilla Custard and Rose Petals, page 108), or 1 large challah
2 cups half-and-half
2 cups heavy cream
Pinch of salt
1 vanilla bean, split lengthwise
6 eggs
1 cup granulated sugar
½ cup orange marmalade, or another jam of your choice
Confectioners' sugar, for dusting

If using homemade brioche, cut the flat brioche loaf horizontally in half, so that you have two flat sheets of bread (or, if using challah, slice it ½ inch thick). Use a cookie cutter to cut out rounds of bread that will fit snugly into the ramekins. You can make additional rounds by cutting half-moons around the edges of a slice of bread, then assembling them into whole rounds later. Place the bread rounds in a baking dish or a sheet pan with sides.

In a saucepan, heat the half-and-half, cream, salt, and vanilla bean over medium heat, stirring occasionally to make sure the mixture doesn't burn or stick to the bottom of the pan. When the cream mixture reaches a fast simmer (do not let it boil), turn off the heat. Set the mixture aside to infuse for 10 minutes.

In a large mixing bowl, whisk the eggs and sugar together. Whisking constantly, gradually add the hot cream mixture. Strain into a large bowl to smooth the mixture and remove the vanilla bean. Pour over the bread rounds and let them soak for 15 minutes, gently turning the bread over once.

Fill the ramekins halfway with soaked bread rounds Spoon a tablespoon of marmalade into each ramekin, then top off with more bread rounds. If there is any remaining custard, pour it into the ramekins until they are almost full. Let the puddings soak in the refrigerator for another 30 minutes.

Heat the oven to 350 degrees. Arrange the ramekins in the hot-water bath. Bake until the puddings are just set and very light golden brown on top, 25 to 30 minutes. Dust the tops with confectioners' sugar and return the puddings to the oven for 10 more minutes to caramelize slightly. Serve warm or chilled.

tasting trio

Coconut–
Pistachio Tuiles

Peanut Butterballs

Bread Puddings
with Orange
Marmalade

Meringue Cigarettes ◎ Chocolate–Caramel Cigarillos

Crunchy Chocolate Haystacks

Myrna's Toasted Coconut–Chocolate Bars

Chocolate Easter Eggs

Coffee Suckers on Cinnamon Sticks

Ruby Raspberry Jellies ◎ Pansy Petal Lollipops

Chewy Butter Caramels

Orange–Honey-Glazed Almonds ◎ Peanut Butterballs

Peppermint Stick–White Chocolate Bark

Sesame Brittle ◎ Chocolate–Mint Tiddlywinks

Cinnamon Peanut Brittle ◎ Chocolate Chews

Peanut–Raisin Chocolate *Rochers* ◎ Patriotic Popcorn Balls

candy BITES

meringue cigarettes

MAKES ABOUT 100

When we opened Tru, it was still unusual for a restaurant to be completely nonsmoking. A few guests lamented the policy, so I started making crisp white meringue cigarettes to have on hand for them. But it turned out that even nonsmokers crave candy cigarettes: Every table wanted them. These even have "filter tips" made from melted chocolate—reminiscent of the candy cigarettes I bought as a child at a local dime store.

You'll need to start these a day ahead.

you'll need

- A pastry bag fitted with a small (¼-inch) plain tip
- A large cookie sheet lined with parchment paper or with nonstick baking mats (see page 16); or a nonstick cookie sheet

½ cup egg whites (from about 4 eggs), at room temperature
½ cup granulated sugar, plus 2 cups extra for serving
⅓ cup confectioners' sugar, sifted
4 ounces milk chocolate
Red food coloring

The day before you plan to serve, start the cigarettes: Turn the oven to 300 degrees and let it heat for at least 20 minutes.

Whip the egg whites in a mixer fitted with a whisk attachment (or using a hand mixer) until foamy. Add the ½ cup of granulated sugar and continue whipping until the whites are stiff and glossy. Add the confectioners' sugar and whip very briefly, just until incorporated (8 to 10 seconds). Spoon the meringue into the pastry bag. Turn off the oven.

Pipe long lines of meringue along the length of the pan, spacing the rows ½ inch apart. (You'll cut these into sections to make the cigarettes.) After the oven has been off for at least 5 minutes, place the pan in the oven. Close the door and let the meringues dry out overnight, until crisp.

Melt the chocolate (see page 11). Pour about 2 cups of granulated sugar into a bowl, making it at least 2 inches deep. Using a serrated knife with a sawing motion, cut the meringue into 3½-inch-long sections.

Dip 1 inch of the end of each cigarette in the melted chocolate to make the "filter." Stick the clean end of the cigarette in the sugar to hold it up while the chocolate sets. When the chocolate is set, drip a few drops of red food coloring onto a paper towel and dab the very tip of the clean end of each cigarette, making it look like the cigarette has been lit. Serve the cigarettes on a tray or stuck into the bowl of sugar, to look like an ashtray.

tasting trio

Root Beer Slush in Vanilla Cream Cordial Cups

Chocolate–Caramel Cigarillos

Meringue Cigarettes

chocolate–caramel cigarillos

MAKES 30

These chewy little chocolate–caramel sticks are just irresistible. I loved chocolate cigarettes as a kid, but the sight of children pretending to smoke doesn't seem quite as innocent as it used to (although I ate packs and packs of candy cigarettes and never became a smoker!). I like to serve these to adults together with my Meringue Cigarettes (page 130), all stuck into a bowl of sugar to look like those elegant old hotel ashtrays.

You'll need to start these the day before serving.

you'll need

- A 10 x 10-inch (or larger) baking pan, lined with plastic wrap
- An offset spatula
- A cookie sheet, oiled

FOR THE CHOCOLATE

12 ounces semisweet chocolate
½ cup light corn syrup
¾ teaspoon warm water

FOR THE CARAMEL

1¼ cups granulated sugar
1½ tablespoons unsalted butter
¼ cup heavy cream, warmed
¾ teaspoon pure orange extract (see Sources, page 300)
⅛ teaspoon salt
Confectioners' sugar, for rolling

Make the chocolate: Melt the chocolate (see page 11). Add the corn syrup and water, stir well, and scrape into the lined baking pan. The mixture should be about ⅛ inch thick in the pan, but it might not fill the pan completely; spread the mixture out with the offset spatula until smooth. Cover with plastic wrap and let the chocolate set overnight at room temperature; it will be stiff but still flexible.

Also the day before, make the caramel: Pour the granulated sugar into the center of a deep saucepan. Carefully pour ½ cup water around the walls of the pan, trying not to splash any sugar onto the walls. Do not stir; gently draw your finger twice through the center of the sugar, making a cross, to moisten it. Over high heat, bring to a full boil and cook without stirring, swirling the pan occasionally to even out the color, until the mixture is amber-caramel in color, 10 to 20 minutes. Immediately turn off the heat and use a wooden spoon to slowly and carefully stir in the butter, then the cream and the extract (it will bubble up and may splatter). Pour the caramel onto the oiled cookie sheet and let it sit at room temperature until firm.

When ready to make the cigarillos, turn the chocolate out onto a work surface dusted with confectioners' sugar and peel off the plastic wrap. Working in 2 batches if needed, roll the chocolate out until smooth and thin, dusting the rolling pin with confectioners' sugar. Cut it into small rectangles, about 3 × ¾ inches. Cut the caramel into strips and roll the strips into "worms" 3 inches long and ¼ inch thick. Wrap each chocolate rectangle around a caramel "worm" to make tiny chocolate-covered cigars.

tasting trio

Peanut Butter Cookie–Grape Jelly Ice Cream Sandwiches

Clementines in Mint Syrup

Chocolate–Caramel Cigarillos

crunchy chocolate haystacks

MAKES 15 TO 20

Dense, rich chocolate and anything light, airy, and crunchy always make a great combination. These little mounds couldn't be easier to make, and you'll find them even easier to munch. Fans of Nestlé's Crunch and Krackle bars will be especially impressed.

you'll need

A large cookie sheet, well greased or lined with parchment paper or with nonstick baking mats (see page 16); or a nonstick cookie sheet

8 ounces semisweet chocolate
¾ cup corn flakes or crushed thin, light wafer cookies such as *gaufrettes* (European waffle cookies)
¼ cup flaked sweetened coconut, toasted (see page 12), optional

Melt the chocolate (see page 11). Remove the chocolate from the heat and stir in the corn flakes and coconut, if using. Mound the mixture in teaspoons onto the cookie sheet, piling it up to make the mounds as high as possible. Let the haystacks set until firm (you can speed up the process by putting the pan in the refrigerator). Store in an airtight container.

myrna's toasted coconut–chocolate bars

MAKES 50

This recipe, inspired by childhood conflict over the relative merits of Mounds and Almond Joy candy bars, can actually make both. My mother adored all things coconut; the flaked sweetened kind was still quite new and exotic when I was little. She was a Mounds girl, but you can press a whole blanched almond into each fragrant coconut bar before you bake them, like I like.

you'll need

Two cookie sheets, well greased or lined with parchment paper or with nonstick baking mats (see page 16); or nonstick cookie sheets—one for baking and one for setting the chocolate

Heaping ¾ cup sugar
Scant ½ cup egg whites (from about 3 eggs)
12 ounces sweetened flaked coconut
12 ounces semisweet chocolate
About 50 whole blanched almonds (optional)

Heat the oven to 350 degrees.

Mix the sugar, egg whites, and coconut in a medium bowl until well blended. Drop by rounded teaspoonfuls onto one cookie sheet. Using your hands, pinch each coconut mound to form it into a small bar. If using almonds, press one gently into the top of each bar. Bake until light golden brown, about 10 minutes. Let the bars cool.

Melt the chocolate (see page 11).

Working one at a time, drop the coconut bars into the chocolate and fish them out with a fork, shaking lightly to allow some of the excess chocolate to drip off. Place on the second cookie sheet and let the chocolate set until firm. Store in an airtight container for up to one week.

tasting trio

Clementines in Mint Syrup

Profiteroles with Caramel Caps

Myrna's Toasted Bars

chocolate easter eggs

MAKES 8 TO 10

Colorful home-dyed Easter eggs are so beautiful, but I was always disappointed as a child after a long hunt to find an ordinary hard-boiled egg lurking under that gorgeous shell. So I invented these: Easter eggs worth finding! They're just as much fun to make, and much better for biting into.

If you like, decorate half of these eggs with white polka dots instead of stripes, using a small paintbrush to apply the white chocolate. I love these for a kids' egg hunt, with real eggs hidden outside and the chocolate ones, nestled into green "grass" nests made from fluffy coconut, hidden inside.

you'll need

- A plastic container with a tight-fitting lid
- A large cookie sheet lined with parchment paper or with nonstick baking mats (see page 16); or a nonstick cookie sheet

- 12 ounces marzipan
- 10 ounces semisweet chocolate
- ¼ cup dried cherries, chopped
- 4 ounces white chocolate
- Coconut grass (see page 14)

Mix the marzipan until slightly softened in a mixer fitted with a paddle attachment, or a mixing bowl. Coarsely chop 2 ounces of the semisweet chocolate and add it to the marzipan. Add the chopped dried cherries and knead together until well combined. Using your hands, roll the mixture into egg shapes about the size of walnuts. Set the eggs aside on a plate. Cover with plastic wrap and refrigerate for about 1 hour to firm.

Melt the remaining 8 ounces of chocolate (see page 11). Pour about ¼ cup of the melted chocolate into the lidded plastic container. Put one egg in the container and cover tightly. Shake the container to roll the egg around and coat it completely with chocolate. Lift out with your fingers or a fork and transfer to the cookie sheet. Repeat, adding more melted chocolate to the container as needed, until all the eggs are coated. Let the coating set for

10 minutes; if the chocolate has not firmed up, refrigerate for 15 minutes or until set.

Meanwhile, melt the white chocolate over steaming (not simmering) water. Holding a dark-chocolate egg in the middle, dip each end in the white chocolate (leaving the center brown) to make a striped egg. Return to the cookie sheet to set until firm. Serve on nests of coconut grass.

tasting trio

Stained-Glass Cookies

Striped Juice Shots

Chocolate Easter Eggs

coffee suckers on cinnamon sticks

MAKES 12

Many great desserts are born in the pastry kitchen, often because there are just so many fun things to play with: bins of chocolates, spices, and dried fruits; squeeze-bottles full of fruit purées; every shape and size of candy mold and baking dish. One day as I was making lollipops for the dinner service, my eye fell on a bunch of long cinnamon sticks. I remembered a coffee-making trick of tossing a cinnamon stick into the filter while the coffee brews, and something in my brain produced this warm, toasty lollipop.

Cinnamon is the curled bark of the cassia tree, and the sticks can be as long as 3 feet! But any cinnamon sticks, long or stubby, will work in the recipe. See the Sources section (page 300).

you'll need

- 12 large lollipop molds (optional; available at craft and baking supply stores)
- A cookie sheet, well greased or lined with a nonstick baking mat (see page 16)
- A candy thermometer
- A pastry brush
- An ice-water bath (see page 21)

12 cinnamon sticks, about 3 inches long
2 cups sugar
⅓ cup light corn syrup
1 teaspoon coffee extract, or 1 teaspoon instant coffee mixed with 1 teaspoon hot water

If you have lollipop collar molds, fit them with cinnamon sticks and lay on the cookie sheet. Or, just lay out the cinnamon sticks in rows, leaving 2 inches of space between them.

Combine the sugar, corn syrup, and ¾ cup water in a small saucepan (preferably one with a pouring spout) fitted with the candy thermometer and bring to a boil over high heat. Without stirring, cook until the mixture reaches 305 degrees or "hard-crack" stage on the candy thermometer. (While the syrup is cooking, occasionally wash down the sides of the pan with the pastry brush dipped in water, to prevent crystallization.)

When the mixture is done, remove the pot from the heat and dip the bottom of it into the ice bath for 15 seconds to stop the cooking. Remove the pot from the ice bath and gently swirl in the coffee. To avoid air bubbles in the finished lollipops, stir the mixture gently in both directions, but be careful not to overmix. If using lollipop molds, pour or carefully spoon the syrup into the molds, filling them two-thirds full. Or, let the mixture cool slightly to thicken, then gently pour a thick coin of syrup over the end of each cinnamon stick. Let the lollipops cool until hard, at least 20 minutes. Remove them from the molds (if using) and lift them off the pan. Store in an airtight container for up to 1 week, or 2 to 3 days if the weather is very humid.

tasting trio

Baby French Toast with Creamy Blueberry Stuffing

Elsie's Baby Rugelach

Coffee Suckers on Cinnamon Sticks

ruby raspberry jellies

MAKES ABOUT 90

See photograph, page 157

When golden-brown cookies and dark-brown chocolates threaten to overwhelm my *petit-four* trays, I can always depend on the bright garnet sparkle of these candies, lively in color and flavor. In France, where I learned to make them, *gelées* come in a tremendous range of colors and flavors, from grass green kiwi to deep purple blackberry.

Raspberry jellies are one of the few fruit-flavored candies that cooks can make at home without any artificial flavors. The difference really shows. And if you're a fan of Chuckles candies, these will blow your mind. Pectin is a natural fruit gelatin that you can buy in powder form, especially during canning season (June to October). Ascorbic acid, a natural antioxidant available at natural-food stores, keeps the color bright.

you'll need

A candy thermometer

A shallow baking dish, about 8 x 12 inches, lined with plastic wrap

2 cups raspberry purée (about 4 cups fresh or frozen raspberries, puréed and then strained to make 2 cups)

4 teaspoons pectin, available in the baking section of supermarkets or natural-food stores

6 tablespoons plus 2¼ cups sugar, plus extra for rolling

⅜ cup corn syrup

2 teaspoons non-buffered ascorbic acid, available at natural-food stores (or see Sources, page 300)

Heat the raspberry purée over medium-high heat in a saucepan fitted with a candy thermometer. When it reaches 100 degrees, add the pectin and the 6 tablespoons of sugar. Bring to a boil, stirring constantly. Add the 2¼ cups of sugar and the corn syrup and cook until the mixture reaches 225 degrees, stirring slowly and constantly.

Dissolve the ascorbic acid in 1 teaspoon water. Remove the pan from the heat and stir in the ascorbic acid. Pour the mixture into the baking dish and let it set for at least 2 hours or overnight, until gelled and firm. Cut the jelly neatly into 1-inch squares. Spread a few tablespoons of sugar in a dish and roll each square in sugar to coat. Wrap the jellies individually in cellophane or store in an airtight container. At room temperature, they keep up to 4 weeks.

tasting trio

Profiteroles with Caramel Caps

Biscotti Milano

Ruby Raspberry Jellies

pansy petal lollipops

MAKES 10 TO 20

See photograph, page 158

Lollipops are the last thing you expect to see on a *petit-four* tray in a fancy restaurant—so that's why I like to serve them last at mine. People burst out laughing when these jewellike treats arrive on a silver platter after dessert. But then they sit back and savor those suckers right down to the stick! I never get tired of watching Chicago's elegant diners licking lollipops like kids—and taking a last few minutes to enjoy the evening.

Using a very long stick makes these lollipops look and feel more fancy. The flower petals are also very pretty—but optional. If you plan to make these without lollipop molds, just arrange the sticks and petals on the cookie sheet. Let the syrup cool a bit to thicken it slightly, and then pour it over the ends of the sticks.

you'll need

- 10 large or 20 small lollipop molds (optional; available at craft stores and baking supply stores)
- 10 to 20 lollipop sticks, about 7 inches long
- A cookie sheet, well greased or lined with a nonstick baking mat (see page 16)
- A candy thermometer
- A clean pastry brush
- An ice water-bath (see page 21)

- 10 to 20 pansy petals, or other edible flower petals, such as rose or violet (optional)
- 1 cup sugar
- ⅓ cup corn syrup
- 1½ teaspoons pure orange or lemon extract (see Sources, page 300)
- A few drops of orange or yellow food coloring

If you have lollipop collar molds, fit them with sticks and lay them on the prepared pan. Or, just lay out the sticks in rows, leaving 2 inches of space between them. Place a few flower petals in each collar or near the end of each stick (you'll pour the syrup over them to make the lollipops).

Combine the sugar, corn syrup, and ⅓ cup water in a clean, dry small saucepan (preferably one with a pouring spout) fitted with the candy thermometer and bring to a boil over high heat. Without stirring, cook until the mixture reaches 305 degrees or "hard-crack" stage on the candy thermometer. (While the syrup is cooking, occasionally wash down the sides of the pan with the brush dipped in water, to prevent crystallization.)

When the mixture is done, remove the pot from the heat and dip it into the ice-water bath for 15 seconds to stop the cooking. Remove the pot from the ice bath and add the extract, then add drops of food coloring until the color pleases you, stirring very gently with a wooden spoon so that the color is evenly distributed. To avoid air bubbles in the finished lollipops, stir the mixture gently in both directions, but be careful not to overmix.

Pour or carefully spoon the syrup over the flower petals into the molds, filling them two-thirds full. Cool for at least 20 minutes, until hard. Lift the lollipops off the pan and remove them from the molds. Store in an airtight container for up to 1 week, or 2 to 3 days if the weather is very humid.

tasting trio

Lemon Cream Daisies

Striped Juice Shots

Pansy Petal Lollipops

chewy butter caramels

MAKES 32

The first homemade candy I ever tasted was a chewy-smooth caramel, made annually for Halloween by a very popular mother in my neighborhood. We used to swing by her house three or four times, hoping that she didn't recognize our costumes. These have a wonderful pure butter and cream flavor and are very easy to make; you don't even need a candy thermometer.

You can cut these into any shape, but keep them bite-size.

you'll need

A loaf pan, lined with parchment paper or plastic wrap

2½ cups sugar
3 tablespoons unsalted butter
½ cup heavy cream, warmed
¼ teaspoon salt

Pour the sugar into the center of a deep saucepan. Carefully pour ½ cup water around the sugar, trying not to splash any sugar onto the sides of the pot. Do not stir; gently draw your finger through the center of the sugar to moisten it. Over high heat, bring to a full boil and cook without stirring until the mixture is amber-caramel in color, 10 to 20 minutes, swirling the mixture in the pot occasionally to even out the color. When the mixture is done, immediately remove the pot from the heat.

Use a wooden spoon to carefully stir in the butter and then the cream and salt; the mixture will foam up and may splatter. When the caramel is smooth, pour it into the pan and let it cool until firm, 30 minutes to 1 hour. When firm, lift the caramel out of the pan. Use a heavy knife to cut it into strips, then into squares. Wrap in decorative plastic wrap. Store at room temperature.

tasting trio

Chocolate Doughnuts with Vanilla Malteds and Cranberry Jam

Orange–Honey-Glazed Almonds

Caramels

stained-glass cookies *(recipe page 58)*

this page, clockwise, from top left marshmallow moons *(recipe page 40);* white-pepper shortbread cups with blueberries *(recipe page 32);* mah-jongg tiles *(recipe page 24);* chocolate chipless cookies *(recipe page 30)*

this page, clockwise, from top left mint-chocolate-chip meringues *(recipe page 56)*; french macaroons with coffee cream *(recipe page 62)*; thimble cookies *(recipe page 48)*; orange tuiles *(recipe page 60)*

above very red velvet cupcakes *(recipe page 96)* opposite butterfly cupcakes *(recipe page 68)*

devil's peaks with double-chocolate drizzle *(recipe page 76)*

coconut snowballs *(recipe page 70)*

◎ above cannelés *(recipe page 90)* ◎ opposite, from left chockablock chocolate cakes with warm macadamia nut caramel *(recipe page 80)*; tiny lemon angel cakes with lemon confit *(recipe page 83)*

lemon cream daisies *(recipe page 106)*

banana brûlée spoonfuls *(recipe page 118)*

◎ above, from top left clockwise ruby raspberry jellies *(recipe page 140);* orange–honey-glazed almonds *(recipe page 177);* chocolate-mint tiddlywinks *(recipe page 182)* ◎ opposite peppermint stick–white chocolate bark *(recipe page 180)*

above pansy petal lollipops *(recipe page 142)* opposite chocolate seashells and white coffee ice cream pearls *(recipe page 198)*

ice cream mini-cones *(recipe page 194)*

peanut butter cookie-grape jelly ice cream sandwiches *(recipe page 192)*

buttermilk-key lime sherbet in roasted pineapple sleeves *(recipe page 204)*

foreground mini granita watermelons *(recipe page 206)*; background parfaits of tangerine sorbet and sour-cream ice cream *(recipe page 190)* profiterole with caramel caps *(recipe page 201)*

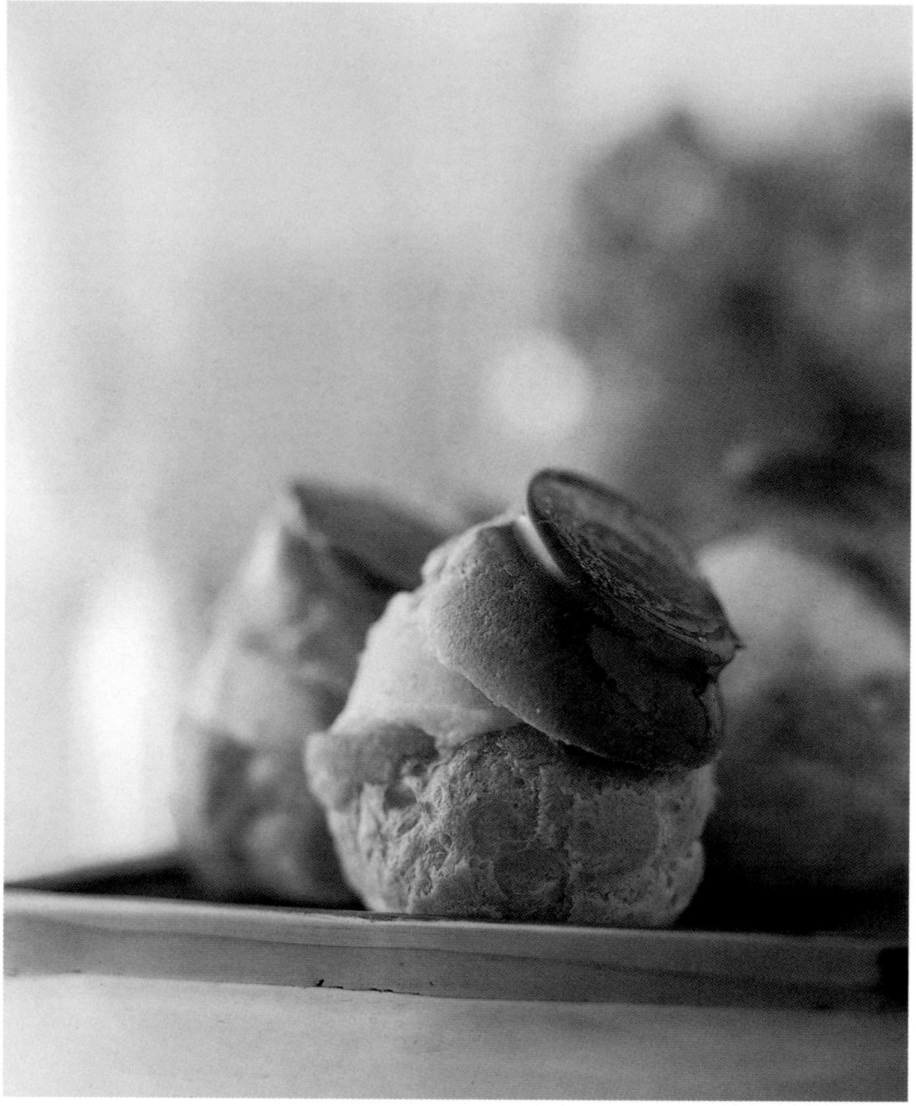

hot chocolate-banana wontons with mango sauce *(recipe page 224)*

◎ above chocolate doughnuts with vanilla malteds and cranberry jam *(recipe page 216)*
◎ opposite, foreground white-hot chocolate *(recipe page 240);* background hot cocoa shots with mini-marshmallows *(recipe page 241)*

clockwise, from above chocolate pots-de-crème with orange whipped cream *(recipe page 234);* chocolate soufflé pots *(recipe page 230);* chocolate-raspberry pot pies *(recipe page 228)*

lemon meringue beehives *(recipe page 252)*

striped juice shots *(recipe page 249)*

above vacherins with raspberries and cream *(recipe page 278)*

opposite taffy lady apples *(recipe page 262)*

petit popovers with peach butter *(recipe page 270)*

blue cheese fritters with pear salad *(recipe page 286)*

bite-size cheesecakes on lemon-pepper-cornmeal crusts *(recipe page 282)*

orange–honey-glazed almonds

MAKES 2 CUPS

See photograph, page 157

I never met a glazed almond I didn't like, but these are my very favorites—spiced with cinnamon, sparked with orange, and with a good shot of honey to sweeten. Don't leave out the salt, which brings out all the other flavors. Anyone who likes honey-roasted nuts will be mad for these. They are particularly excellent with good ripe cheese, whether you're serving it before or after the meal.

Blanched almonds have been dipped in boiling water to remove the brown skins, but you can use almonds with the skins on if you prefer.

you'll need

A large cookie sheet, well greased or lined with nonstick baking mats (see page 16); or a nonstick cookie sheet

- 2 cups whole blanched almonds
- 1/4 teaspoon salt
- 2 tablespoons honey
- 1 teaspoon cinnamon
- Freshly grated zest of 1 orange

Heat the oven to 375 degrees.

Toss all the ingredients together in a bowl, then turn out onto the cookie sheet. Spread out so the almonds do not touch each other. Bake until lightly toasted, 15 to 20 minutes, stirring occasionally to prevent sticking. As they come out of the oven, loosen the almonds from the bottom of the pan with a spatula. Let them cool in the pan.

Let the almonds cool to room temperature, then store them in an airtight container for up to 2 weeks, or less if the weather is very humid.

tasting trio

Green Grapes Glacé

Blue Cheese Fritters with Pear Salad

Orange–Honey-Glazed Almonds

peanut butterballs

MAKES ABOUT 50

To my mind, peanut butter was invented because of how good it is with chocolate. That combination simply had to be, and this is my absolute favorite version of it. If you've never made peanut butter, you'll see that it's nothing more complex than pulsing the nuts in a food processor—but the fresh flavor is fabulous. For this recipe, I stiffen the peanut butter with graham cracker crumbs to make it a bit less sticky and more crumbly, then dip balls of the mixture in plain chocolate. They are very sturdy and travel well.

I know that wars have been waged, lost, and won over the chunky *vs.* smooth peanut butter issue, but for this recipe I come down squarely in the smooth camp. You want a lush, creamy mouthful with a crisp chocolate crust.

you'll need

Two cookie sheets, ungreased

About 50 paper bonbon cups or mini-muffin cups, any color

18 ounces dry-roasted unsalted peanuts
Peanut oil
1 pound confectioners' sugar
1⅓ cups graham cracker crumbs
12 tablespoons (1½ sticks) unsalted butter, at room temperature
12 ounces milk chocolate

Grind the peanuts in a food processor until smooth. If the mixture seems too thick and grainy, add peanut oil a little bit at a time by drizzling a thin stream through the feed tube with the motor running. Purée until the mixture is smooth and the consistency of peanut butter.

Transfer the peanut butter to the bowl of a mixer fitted with a paddle attachment (or any large bowl) and add the confectioners' sugar, graham cracker crumbs, and butter. Mix together until smooth. Form the mixture into bite-size balls and set aside on an ungreased cookie sheet. Chill until slightly firmed, about 30 minutes.

Meanwhile, arrange the paper cups on a cookie sheet. Melt the chocolate (see page 11). Dip the tops of the peanut butter balls into the melted chocolate and set each one, chocolate side up, in a paper cup. Let the chocolate set before serving, about 30 minutes at room temperature (or refrigerate for 10 minutes if you're in a hurry).

Store in an airtight container for up to 1 week.

tasting trio

Caramel–Orange Rice Crisps

Ice Cream Mini-Cones

Peanut Butterballs

peppermint stick–white chocolate bark

MAKES 20 TO 30 PIECES

See photograph, page 156

A confession: This recipe began as a way to use all the candy canes that seem to pour into my house at Christmastime. Regular candy canes are fine, but I especially love the airy, crispy texture of King Leo brand peppermint sticks. Serve this white-and-pink confection on brightly colored plates, or box it up in Chinese takeout containers to give as gifts.

The peppermint oil gives a light additional mintiness, but you may leave it out.

you'll need

A cookie sheet with sides, about 13 x 17 inches, lined with parchment paper or with a nonstick baking mat (see page 16)

8 ounces white chocolate, chopped (see page 11)

8 King Leo-brand red-and-white peppermint sticks or 4 candy canes, about 6 inches long

2 drops peppermint oil or extract (optional; see Sources, page 300)

Melt the chocolate (see page 11).

Place the peppermint sticks in a heavy, resealable plastic bag and crush them fine by whacking and then rolling them with a rolling pin. They should have about the same consistency as crushed ice.

When the chocolate is melted, stir in the peppermint oil. Stir in all but 1 tablespoon of the crushed peppermint pieces and spread the mixture out on the cookie sheet, about ¼ inch thick. It will not fill the pan completely. Sprinkle with the remaining tablespoon of pieces.

Let the mixture harden at room temperature, about 2 hours. (Or, refrigerate for 30 minutes to harden more quickly.) Use your hands to break the bark into pieces. Store in an airtight container for up to 2 weeks.

tasting trio

Mini Root Beer Floats

Marshmallow Moons

Peppermint Stick–White Chocolate Bark

sesame brittle

MAKES 25 TO 35 PIECES

Tiny, toasty sesame seeds make a brittle that's very different from the usual peanut and cashew varieties. This candy gives you the solid crunch of packed sesame in each bite, bathed in the warmth of caramelized sugar.

When you're ready to break up the brittle, wear cotton gloves, surgical gloves, or even plastic baggies on your hands to prevent sticking and fingerprints.

you'll need

A candy thermometer

A cookie sheet with sides, about 13 x 17 inches, well oiled with vegetable oil

¾ cup sesame seeds, toasted (see page 12)
2 cups sugar
¼ teaspoon cream of tartar
1 cup light corn syrup
2 tablespoons unsalted butter

Combine ½ cup water with the sugar, cream of tartar, and corn syrup in a medium-size heavy saucepan fitted with the candy thermometer. Bring to a boil over medium heat. After it boils, stir the mixture occasionally. Boil the mixture until it reaches 350 degrees. The color should be deep golden brown. Remove from the heat and stir in the butter until melted, then stir in the sesame seeds.

Pour the mixture onto the oiled pan and spread it out a bit with the back of a wooden spoon, to about ¼-inch thickness. (If you want a thinner result, place a nonstick baking mat on top of the warm mixture and roll lightly.)

Let the brittle harden, uncovered, in a cool place, 30 to 45 minutes. Using your hands, break the brittle into pieces. Store in an airtight container for up to 1 week, or 3 days if the weather is very humid.

tasting trio

Dried-Plum–Pecan Chews

Parfaits of Tangerine Sorbet and Sour-Cream Ice Cream

Sesame Brittle

chocolate–mint tiddlywinks

MAKES 20

See photograph, page 157

You can't grow up in Chicago without becoming obsessed with the Frango mints sold at Marshall Field's. They're a simple combination of chocolate and mint *ganache*—a pastry term for chocolate and cream mixed together.

This sweet is a dark chocolate disk with a fresh, bright green mint leaf embedded into each one. It's very easy to do, especially if you can find sheets of clear acetate, which lets you see what you are doing at every step. You can use baking mats or even parchment paper if necessary. The chocolate seems to preserve the mint leaf: It will stay green and fresh for 2 or 3 days.

you'll need

2 sheets of acetate, the thicker the better, each about 18 x 24 inches (you can get this at an art supply store), or 2 pieces of parchment paper, or 2 nonstick baking mats

A pastry bag, optional (see page 15)

20 fresh whole mint leaves, unblemished

4 ounces semisweet chocolate

Lay a sheet of acetate or parchment or a nonstick baking mat (smooth side up) on a work surface. Place the mint leaves on the sheet, face down, 2 inches apart.

Melt the chocolate (see page 11). Use a spoon or pastry bag to cover each mint leaf with a teaspoon of melted chocolate. Working carefully, place another sheet of acetate or parchment paper or a baking mat (smooth side down) over the first one. Gently press down directly on top of each leaf to spread the chocolate around the leaf, making a border about ¼ inch wide all around (don't worry if they're not very neat). Let the chocolate set for at least 1 hour, until firm. Gently peel off the acetate.

Store in an airtight container for up to 3 days. Serve with the mint leaves showing.

tasting trio

Chockablock Chocolate Cakes with Warm Macadamia Nut Caramel

Orange Tuiles

Tiddlywinks

cinnamon peanut brittle

MAKES 25 TO 35 PIECES

Adding cinnamon to a traditional peanut brittle really wakes up all the flavors. I always use salted peanuts for brittles, so that the finished candy is an intense salty–sweet–toasty–crunchy bite. This is outrageously good with cool and creamy desserts.

you'll need

A candy thermometer

A cookie sheet with sides, about 13 x 17 inches, well oiled with vegetable oil

2 cups sugar
¼ teaspoon cream of tartar
1 cup light corn syrup
2 teaspoons ground cinnamon
2 tablespoons unsalted butter
2 cups roasted salted peanuts
1 teaspoon baking soda

Combine ½ cup water with the sugar, cream of tartar, and corn syrup in a medium-size heavy saucepan fitted with the candy thermometer. Bring to a boil over medium heat. After it boils, stir occasionally. Boil the mixture until it reaches 340 degrees. The color should be deep golden brown. Remove from the heat and, quickly, stir in the cinnamon with a wooden spoon. Stir in the butter until it is melted, then the peanuts and baking soda.

Pour the mixture onto the oiled pan and spread it out a bit with the back of a wooden spoon, to about ¼-inch thickness (it may not fill the whole pan). Let the brittle harden, uncovered, in a cool place, 30 to 45 minutes.

Using your hands, and wearing cotton or plastic gloves if desired to keep off any fingerprints, break the brittle into pieces. Store in an airtight container.

tasting trio

Frozen Cream–Dark Chocolate Sandwiches

Banana Brûlée Spoonfuls

Cinnamon Peanut Brittle

chocolate chews

MAKES ABOUT 75 PIECES

I've always loved the chewy texture and the chocolatey, surprisingly orange-tinged flavor of Tootsie Rolls. So imagine my surprise when I learned that the basic formula is so simple: melted chocolate mixed with corn syrup. Pastry chefs have long used this combination, which takes on a plasticine-like texture, as a kind of moldable chocolate. It lasts almost forever and is incredibly easy to shape into roses, roll into sheets, form into a child's initials—whatever you can think of.

These make a glamorous presentation when wrapped in gold paper.

you'll need

A cookie sheet with sides, about 13 x 17 inches, lined with plastic wrap

About 75 squares of colored foil or cellophane, for wrapping (optional)

12 ounces semisweet chocolate
½ cup light corn syrup
¾ teaspoon warm water
1½ teaspoons orange extract (see Sources, page 300)

Melt the chocolate (see page 11). Add the remaining ingredients, stir well, and scrape into the prepared pan. The mixture should be about 1 inch thick in the pan; it will not fill the pan entirely. Cover and let the mixture set overnight at room temperature; it will be stiff but still flexible.

Turn the candy out onto a work surface. Cut into ¾-inch-wide strips, then use your hands to "scrunch" each strip into a log. Roll the logs thin between your hands (or on the work surface) until they are about ½ inch in diameter. Cut into 1-inch-long sections. Set aside the candies to firm up a bit before wrapping or serving (the mixture warms up and softens as you handle it).

Roll each candy up in a square of colored foil or cellophane, twisting the ends to secure.

tasting trio

Coconut Whiteout Cakes

Vanilla-Crusted Strawberries

Chocolate Chews

peanut–raisin chocolate *rochers*

MAKES ABOUT 20

One of my favorite things about being a pastry chef is having the tools (and a good excuse) to re-create the things I loved to eat when I was little. You have only to look at the ingredients list to realize that this is a bite-size rendition of a Chunky chocolate bar, a personal favorite. These are actually a rather adult bite, loaded with crunchy peanuts and chewy, intense raisins. You can use any nut–fruit combination you like.

Rochers, or rocks, are a classic item of French confectionery. They look like little Flintstones-style boulders, which is why I like to serve them nestled into a bed of "grass" made of shredded coconut tossed with green food coloring.

you'll need

A large cookie sheet, well greased or lined with parchment paper or with nonstick baking mats (see page 16); or a nonstick cookie sheet

8 ounces milk chocolate, roughly chopped (see page 11)
½ cup raw peanuts, lightly toasted (see page 12), cooled, and roughly chopped
½ cup raisins
Coconut grass (see page 14)

Melt the chocolate (see page 11). When it is melted, remove it from the heat and mix in the peanuts and raisins.

Drop the mixture by teaspoonfuls onto the cookie sheet, using a finger to push each spoonful off the spoon in a mounded "boulder" shape. Let the chocolate set at room temperature until firm and completely cooled. Store in an airtight container for up to 1 week.

tasting trio

Ice Cream Mini-Cones

Caramel–Orange Rice Crisps

Peanut–Raisin Chocolate *Rochers*

patriotic popcorn balls

MAKES 12

It isn't a real July Fourth for me without a red, white, and blue confection on the table, just for fun. Smooth white chocolate is perfect for making crunchy popcorn balls; it doesn't get very hot, so you can form the balls while the chocolate is melted without burning your hands. I add confetti-like red and blue sprinkles inside and out.

Feel free to change the colors as easily as you buy a jar of sprinkles—using school colors, team colors, holiday colors, or none at all. Buy the tiny hard, round kind of sprinkles for this project; the soft, thin ones will melt. If you have lollipop sticks on hand, you can turn these into popcorn-on-a-stick by inserting the sticks while the balls are still warm. And the balls look great wrapped in colored cellophane, tied with a silvery cord.

you'll need
A muffin tin

2 tablespoons *each* red and blue sprinkles (the hard round kind, not the long thin kind), or red and blue sugar
8 ounces white chocolate, chopped
4 cups popped popcorn, salted

Line the muffin tin with plastic wrap by placing a large sheet (or two, if needed) on top and lightly pushing down into the cups. Mix the sprinkles together. Sprinkle half of the mixed sprinkles into the lined cups.

Melt the white chocolate in a large double boiler over barely simmering water, stirring occasionally. Remove from the heat and carefully stir in the popcorn, coating it evenly with melted chocolate. Mix in almost all the remaining sprinkles, reserving some to sprinkle on at the end.

Working quickly, pull off a handful (about ⅓ cup) of coated popcorn and form into a loose ball slightly larger than a golf ball. Place in a lined muffin cup to set. Repeat with the remaining popcorn.

Sprinkle the remaining sprinkles over the popcorn balls. Let them set at room temperature or, for faster results, in the refrigerator. Store in an airtight container for up to 1 week.

tasting trio

Frozen Cream–Dark Chocolate Sandwiches

Striped Juice Shots

Patriotic Popcorn Balls

Parfaits of Tangerine Sorbet and Sour-Cream Ice Cream

Peanut Butter Cookie–Grape Jelly Ice Cream Sandwiches

Ice Cream Mini-Cones ◎ Bomb Poppers

Vanilla Snow with Maple Syrup

Chocolate Seashells and White Coffee Ice Cream Pearls

Profiteroles with Caramel Caps

Buttermilk–Key Lime Sherbet in Roasted Pineapple Sleeves

Mini Granita Watermelons

Nutmeg Ice Cream with Gingerbread Wafers

Mini Root Beer Floats

Root Beer Slush–Vanilla Cream Cordial Cups

frozen BITES

parfaits of tangerine sorbet and sour-cream ice cream

MAKES 10

See photograph, page 163

The flavor combination of the Creamsicle has haunted me for years. As I child I was convinced that mixing orange juice and milk in a glass would achieve the same effect, and couldn't understand why the milk curdled every single time! Then I discovered the genius of the Orange Julius (orange juice mixed with melted vanilla ice cream) and proceeded from there to this parfait. It is wonderfully refreshing, and I must say that it is even better than a Creamsicle, at least to a grown-up's taste.

you'll need

- An ice-water bath (see page 21)
- A candy thermometer (optional)
- An ice-cream machine
- 10 small clear decorative glasses, for serving

FOR THE SORBET

½ cup sugar
2 cups tangerine juice
¼ cup fresh lemon juice

FOR THE ICE CREAM

1½ cups milk
⅔ cup sugar
4 egg yolks
½ cup sour cream

Make the sorbet: Place a bowl in the freezer to chill. Combine 1 cup water with the sugar in a saucepan and bring to a boil. Whisk the juices together in another bowl. Let the sugar syrup cool slightly, then whisk half the syrup into the juices and taste. Slowly add more syrup, tasting frequently. The mixture should taste definitely tart and sweet; you might not use all the syrup. Freeze in the ice-cream machine, then transfer to the frozen bowl and keep frozen.

Make the ice cream: Prepare an ice-water bath.

Combine the milk with ⅓ cup of the sugar in a saucepan and heat just to a boil. Immediately remove from the heat.

Whisk the egg yolks with the remaining ⅓ cup of sugar until well combined. Whisk a few tablespoons of the hot milk mixture into the egg mixture, then pour back into the saucepan with the remaining milk mixture. Place the thermometer, if using, in the mixture.

Cook over medium heat, stirring constantly with a wooden spoon. At 160 degrees, the mixture will give off a puff of steam. When the mixture reaches 180 degrees it will be thickened and creamy, like eggnog. If you're not using a thermometer, test it by dipping a wooden spoon into the mixture. Run your finger down the back of the spoon. If the stripe remains clear, the mixture is ready; if the edges blur, the mixture is not quite thick enough yet. When it is ready, quickly remove it from the heat. Strain the mixture into a bowl and rest the bottom of the bowl in the ice bath to cool. Let the mixture cool, stirring often. When it is cold, whisk in the sour cream and freeze in the ice-cream machine.

To assemble, let both mixtures soften slightly (if needed to scoop them). Scoop into the glasses in striped layers (try to make at least 2 layers of each). Or, pack into Popsicle molds and insert wooden sticks to make pops.

tasting trio

Very Red Velvet Cupcakes

Chocolate–Mint Tiddlywinks

Parfaits of Sorbet and Sour-Cream Ice Cream

peanut butter cookie–grape jelly ice cream sandwiches

MAKES ABOUT 60

See photograph, page 161

Peanut butter and jelly for dessert: a childhood dream come true. Peanut butter's salty–sweet combination makes it a great addition to desserts, at least to those of us who are raised on the stuff. In fact, both peanut butter and grape jelly are distinctively American ingredients. Our purple Concord grapes grow only in America, and we are known around the world for our love of peanut butter!

Grape jams and jellies (like grape juice) get their distinctive deep purple color from the skins of the grapes. Jam works better than jelly in this recipe. Instead of mixing the jam into the ice cream, swirl it in to create sweet, juicy streaks. They're great with the salty, nutty crunch of peanut butter cookies.

you'll need

- Two cookie sheets, well greased or lined with parchment paper or with nonstick baking mats (see page 16); or nonstick cookie sheets
- A mini-ice-cream scoop or a melon baller

FOR THE COOKIES

- 8 tablespoons (1 stick) cool unsalted butter, cut into pieces
- ½ cup granulated sugar
- ½ cup (packed) light brown sugar
- 1 egg
- ½ teaspoon pure vanilla extract
- 1½ cups all-purpose flour
- ¾ teaspoon baking soda
- ¼ teaspoon salt
- ½ cup peanut butter, chunky or smooth

FOR THE ICE CREAM

- 1 pint vanilla ice cream, store-bought or homemade
- ½ cup grape jam, at room temperature

Make the cookies: Cream the butter until smooth and fluffy in a mixer fitted with a paddle attachment. Add both sugars and mix well. Add the egg and vanilla and mix. Sift the flour with the baking soda and salt, then add it to the mixer in two or three batches, mixing after each addition. Add the peanut butter and mix well.

Heat the oven to 400 degrees. Roll the cookie dough into 1-inch balls and place on the cookie sheets 1 inch apart. Press down twice on each cookie with the back of a fork, flattening it on the pan and making a crisscross pattern on top. Bake until light golden brown, 5 to 8 minutes. Let the cookies cool on the pan.

Make the ice ream: Scoop the vanilla ice cream into a bowl and let it soften at room temperature until it is just soft enough to mix. (Or, if making your own ice cream, scoop the ice cream into a frozen bowl as it comes out of the machine.) Fold the grape jam into the ice cream with a rubber spatula, leaving streaks through the ice cream. Don't try to mix it all the way in; you're looking for a swirl effect. Freeze until firm.

To make the sandwiches, turn half of the cookies over so that the smooth side faces up. Place a mini-scoop of ice cream on each, then top with the remaining cookies, so that the crisscross side faces out on both sides of the sandwich. Freeze until ready to serve.

tasting trio

Tangerine Marmalade Babycakes

Chocolate Chews

Peanut Butter Cookie–Grape Jelly Ice Cream Sandwiches

ice cream mini-cones

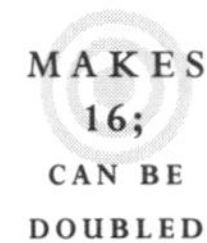
MAKES 16; CAN BE DOUBLED

See photograph, page 160

Any ice cream looks and tastes even better in a thin, crisp crust. These little cones are another version of *tuiles,* thin cookies that are warm and pliable when they come out of the oven, then cool to a crisp crunch. To fill them, you will get the best results from a melon baller or a small-size ice cream scoop. Bring the empty cones to the table on a linen-lined platter, then top with fresh ice cream to order and serve wrapped in a cocktail napkin. Using two or three different ice creams makes this dessert even more charming.

If you'd rather make little crunchy cups that can stand on their own, there's no need for a stencil: just spread the batter into 3-inch circles on the pans. After the baking, lift the tuiles off the pans and gently lower them into shot glasses or mini-muffin cups, pressing them into the cup as though lining a pan with pie dough.

you'll need

- The lid of a disposable plastic container or tub, about 5 inches across
- An offset spatula
- Two cookie sheets, very well greased or lined with nonstick baking mats (see page 16); or 2 high-quality nonstick cookie sheets
- A mini-ice-cream scoop or melon baller

- 2 egg whites, at room temperature
- 6 tablespoons unsalted butter, at room temperature
- ¼ cup sugar
- ½ cup flour, sifted
- ¼ teaspoon pure vanilla extract
- Sorbets and ice creams, for serving

To make a stencil for the cone shape, trace a circle 6 inches across on a piece of paper. Using a pencil and a ruler, divide it evenly into quarters. Cut out one of the quarters. On the plastic lid, trace around the quarter and cut it out with an X-Acto knife or sharp scissors. You now have your stencil: a plastic lid with a quarter-circle cut out of it.

Whip the egg whites in a mixer fitted with a whisk attachment until stiff. Refrigerate the egg whites until ready to use.

Cream the butter in a mixer fitted with a whisk attachment until very smooth. Add the sugar and continue mixing. Add the flour and blend, then add the vanilla and blend. Add the chilled egg whites and mix at low speed just until incorporated.

Heat the oven to 350 degrees. Using the offset spatula, spread a thin layer of batter through the stencil onto one of the cookie sheets. Move the stencil and repeat with the remaining batter.

Bake the tuiles until golden, about 8 minutes. Remove the pans from the oven and leave the oven on. Immediately roll the tuiles into cones: Lift one off the pan with a spatula. Gently bring the straight edges together, overlapping a bit to seal, and pinch the bottom closed. Set aside and repeat with the remaining tuiles. If the tuiles cool too much to bend, return them to the oven for a few moments to soften up. Let the shaped cones cool completely on a wire rack.

When ready to serve, top the cones at the table with mini-scoops of ice cream or sorbet.

tasting trio

Peppermint Stick–White Chocolate Bark

Tiny Lemon Angel Cakes with Lemon Confit

Ice Cream Mini-Cones

bomb poppers

MAKES 15

Frozen juice Popsicles are standard kid fare, but miniature pops of vivid pink, purple, and orange stripes are something quite special. The homemade strawberry juice at the top of the pop is the best part.

You can use anything from toothpicks to long, thin skewers as your stick, as long as it is thin enough to stick into the raspberry at the heart of the pop. The raspberry serves to hold the stick up straight as the mixture freezes.

you'll need

15 stiff paper bonbon cups or small paper cups

15 toothpicks, lollipop sticks, or other small skewers

1 cup strawberries, trimmed and cut up
1 tablespoon sugar
15 raspberries
1 cup orange–banana or plain orange juice
1 cup purple grape juice

Purée the strawberries and sugar together in a blender or food processor. Pass the purée through a strainer to remove the seeds.

Place one raspberry in each paper cup and stab it through the center with a toothpick (don't stab through the cup). Arrange the cups on a tray or in a shallow dish. Pour in the orange-banana juice, dividing it evenly among the cups. Make sure the toothpicks are standing up straight. Freeze until hard, about 3 hours.

Pour in the strawberry purée, dividing it evenly among the cups, and freeze until hard. Repeat with the grape juice.

To eat, peel off the paper cup and hold the popper by the toothpick.

tasting trio

Butterfly Cupcakes
Chocolate Chews
Bomb Poppers

vanilla snow with maple syrup

MAKES 6 TO 8 SERVINGS

In one of my favorite childhood books, a city girl goes to live with relatives in the wilds of northern Vermont. In early spring, the farmers boil the maple tree sap right in the middle of the woods, in a huge kettle. Kids get to ladle the hot syrup onto the snow, where it hardens into a chewy taffy that they stuff, still covered with crunchy ice crystals, into their mouths.

Needless to say, I dreamed about this treat for years, then developed this recipe for hot maple syrup poured on vanilla *granita,* a shaved Italian ice. Kids love it for a winter party. The syrup must be hot in order to achieve the chewiness of taffy, and only real maple syrup will work. You can use Mother Nature's granita, if you prefer: real snow!

you'll need

A shallow baking dish

6 to 8 small serving bowls (not plastic), frozen

6 tablespoons sugar

½ vanilla bean, split

1 cup maple syrup

Combine 2 cups water with the sugar and vanilla bean in a small saucepan and bring to a boil. Set aside for 15 minutes, then pour the mixture into the shallow baking dish. Let the mixture cool to room temperature, then freeze until hard. *(The recipe can be made up to this point and kept frozen for up to 3 days.)*

Using the side of a large sturdy spoon, scrape the surface of the frozen ice to shave it into "snow." Transfer to the frozen bowls and keep frozen until the last minute (it will melt quickly when removed from the freezer).

When ready to serve, bring the maple syrup to a boil in a small saucepan and let it boil for 30 seconds. Immediately remove the pan from the heat and use a spoon to drizzle maple syrup over the vanilla ice. The syrup will harden slightly and become chewy. Serve immediately.

tasting trio

Devil's Peaks with Double-Chocolate Drizzle

Coconut Snowballs

Vanilla Snow with Maple Syrup

chocolate seashells with white coffee ice cream pearls

MAKES 20

See photograph, page 159)

Jim Graham is one of the best *chocolatiers* in the business. It was he who taught me to make this extraordinary pale ivory ice cream that packs the flavor punch of dark-roast espresso. I'll never forget his explanation of how the cream is infused with coffee beans that are then strained out, leaving behind a surprisingly intense "flavor memory" of their presence.

The ice cream is wonderful with anything chocolate, but I urge you to have a little fun with these chocolate seashells. They are beautiful and impressive even when they're not perfect (think of the messy whorls and ridges of an oyster shell). The method is truly easy, and the finished product may be the most impressive dessert in the book.

You can also fill your shells with any white ice cream (or even white chocolate mousse). Start a day ahead if you're making the ice cream.

you'll need

- An ice-water bath (see page 21)
- A candy thermometer (optional)
- An ice-cream machine
- 20 clean seashell halves with smooth insides, such as cherrystone clam
- A mini-ice-cream scoop or spoon

FOR THE ICE CREAM

¼ cup whole dark-roasted coffee beans
2 cups half-and-half
2 cups heavy cream
½ vanilla bean, split lengthwise
8 egg yolks
¾ cup sugar

TO FINISH

8 ounces semisweet chocolate
Raw sugar for serving

At least one day before serving, start the ice cream: Heat the coffee beans, half-and-half, cream, and vanilla bean in a saucepan over medium heat just to a boil, stirring occasionally to make sure the mixture doesn't burn or stick to the bottom of the pan. Turn off the heat and let the mixture cool. Cover it and refrigerate overnight to infuse the coffee flavor.

The next day prepare the ice-water bath.

Whisk the egg yolks and sugar together in a bowl. Strain the vanilla and coffee beans out of the cream mixture and rewarm it in a heavy saucepan. When the cream mixture reaches a fast simmer (do not let it boil), turn off the heat. In a thin stream, whisk half of the cream mixture into the egg yolk mixture. Then pour the remaining half in and whisk well.

Pour the mixture back into the saucepan. Place the thermometer, if using, in the mixture. Cook over medium heat, stirring constantly with a wooden spoon. At 160 degrees, the mixture will give off a puff of steam. When the mixture reaches 180 degrees it will be thickened and creamy, like eggnog. If you're not using a thermometer, test it by dipping a wooden spoon into the mixture. Run your finger down the back of the spoon. If the stripe remains clear, the mixture is ready; if the edges blur, the mixture is not quite thick enough yet. When it is ready, quickly remove it from the heat.

Pour the cream mixture through a fine sieve into a bowl. Rest the bottom of the bowl in the ice bath. Let the mixture cool for 2 hours, stirring occasionally, then freeze it according to the directions for the ice-cream machine.

Make the chocolate shells: Cut pieces of aluminum foil large enough to more than cover the back side of each shell. Cover the back (outside) of each shell with foil, folding it over the rim to hook it tightly to the shell. Press the foil against the surface, rubbing to smooth it so that it is like a skin for the shell. Arrange the wrapped shells on a pan, with the wrapped sides facing up.

Melt the chocolate (page 11). Spoon 1 to 2 tablespoons of chocolate onto the wrapped side of one shell, spreading it with the back of the spoon to

recipe continues on next page

cover the shell all the way to the edge. As needed, add more chocolate until the entire back of the shell is well coated with chocolate. Repeat with the remaining shells and chocolate. Refrigerate the shells until set, 20 to 30 minutes.

Once the chocolate is set, carefully unhook the foil from all around the rim of the shell. Lift the real shell out of the foil, leaving the chocolate-covered foil cups. Carefully peel the foil back to reveal the chocolate shell. Repeat with the remaining shells. Store in an airtight container until ready to serve. *(The shells can be made up to 1 week in advance.)*

To serve, pour raw sugar on a platter to look like sand. Place a scoop of ice cream in each clam shell and rest the shells on the sand. Serve immediately.

tasting trio

Cinnamon Peanut Brittle

Blackberry Brown-Butter Financiers

Chocolate Seashells with Ice Cream Pearls

profiteroles with caramel caps

MAKES
12 TO 15

See photograph, page 164

Two French desserts I love are *profiteroles* and *croquembouche;* I like the names almost as much as the tastes! This is a combination of the two. I take the cream puff and ice cream from the profiteroles, then add the caramel drizzle from the croquembouche (the word means "crunch-in-mouth" in French). Sporting a firm amber lid of candied sugar, each profiterole is a mouthful of tender pastry, ice cream, and crackly caramel.

You can serve three profiteroles together on a plate; they form a smooth caramel plateau that's perfect for holding an extra scoop of ice cream. Or just serve them plain; they're more "pop-able" that way.

you'll need

- A pastry bag fitted with a large plain tip (optional; see page 15)
- Two cookie sheets, well greased or lined with parchment paper or with nonstick baking mats (see page 16); or nonstick cookie sheets
- A pastry brush
- An ice-water bath (see page 21)
- A mini-ice-cream scoop or a melon baller

FOR THE CREAM PUFFS

- 8 tablespoons (1 stick) unsalted butter
- ½ teaspoon salt
- 1½ teaspoons sugar
- 1 cup all-purpose flour
- 5 eggs

FOR THE CARAMEL

- 1¼ cups sugar

TO FINISH

- Ice cream of your choice, or lightly sweetened whipped cream

Make the cream puffs: Heat the oven to 425 degrees.

Combine 1 cup water with the butter, salt, and sugar in a large saucepan and bring to a rolling boil over medium-high heat. When it boils, immediately take the pan off the heat. Stirring with a wooden spoon, add all the flour at once and stir hard until all the flour is incorporated, 30 to 60 sec-

recipe continues on next page

onds. Return the pan to the heat and cook, stirring, 2 minutes to evaporate some of the moisture.

Scrape the mixture into a mixer fitted with a paddle attachment (or use a hand mixer). Mix at medium speed. With the mixer running, and adding 1 egg at a time, add 3 of the eggs, stopping after each addition to scrape down the sides of the bowl. Mix until the dough is smooth and glossy and the eggs are completely incorporated. The dough should be thick, but should fall slowly and steadily from the beaters when you lift them out of the bowl. If the dough is still clinging to the beaters, add another egg and mix until completely incorporated.

Using the pastry bag, pipe the dough in bite-size "kisses" (about 1½ inches across) onto one of the cookie sheets.

Whisk the remaining egg with 1½ teaspoons water. Brush the surface of the puffs with egg wash to smooth out any bumps (you might not use all the egg wash). Bake 15 minutes, then reduce the heat to 375 degrees and bake until the cream puffs are puffed up and light golden brown, about 25 minutes more. Try not to open the oven door too often during the baking. Let the cream puffs cool on the baking sheet.

To make the caramel, pour the 1¼ cups of sugar into the center of a deep saucepan. Carefully pour ⅓ cup water around the sugar, trying not to splash any sugar onto the sides of the pan. Do not stir; gently draw your finger through the center of the sugar to moisten it. Over high heat, bring to a full boil and cook without stirring, swirling the pot occasionally to even out the color, until amber-caramel in color, 10 to 20 minutes. When the mixture is done, remove the pot from the heat and rest the bottom in the ice bath for 15 seconds to stop the cooking.

Dip the top of each cream puff in the caramel and place it caramel-side down, with the base sticking straight up, on the other cookie sheet. The caramel will pool slightly around the puff and will harden. (When you turn the puffs over later, this will be a smooth, flat "lid" for each profiterole.) Let them cool until the caramel is set, at least 10 minutes.

When ready to serve, carefully turn the puffs over and cut each one horizontally in half using a long serrated knife. Fill each with a small scoop of ice cream. Place the lid on top and serve immediately.

tasting trio

Myrna's Toasted Coconut–Chocolate Bars

Peachy Upside-Down Cakes

Profiteroles

buttermilk–key lime sherbet in roasted pineapple sleeves

MAKES ABOUT 40

As fancy new sorbets have taken over in the freezer case, poor sherbet has been shoved aside. Orange and rainbow flavors are about all you can find these days, and they're usually packed with dyes and additives. Sherbet deserves a little respect! Unlike fruit-and-water sorbets, sherbet contains a little bit of milk, which gives it a nice smooth texture—but adds only a speck of fat. Buttermilk and Key lime make a tangy sherbet that you just can't stop eating. (Key limes have a smoother, more floral juice than regular limes.)

Serve this citrusy sherbet with thin slices of mellow roasted pineapple, which is full of natural fruit sugars. I caramelize the pineapple whole almost like making a roast: Brown it all over, then slow-bake until cooked all the way through. Try to slice it very, very thin, so that you can drape it around the sherbet. But chunks of roasted pineapple topped with this sherbet taste wonderful too.

You'll need to start this a day ahead.

you'll need

An ice-cream machine

FOR THE PINEAPPLE

4 tablespoons unsalted butter
¼ cup (packed) light brown sugar
1 vanilla bean, split lengthwise
1 pineapple, peeled and left whole

FOR THE SHERBET

1 cup sugar
2 cups buttermilk
½ cup Key lime juice, fresh or bottled

Make the pineapple: The day before you plan to serve the dessert, melt the butter over medium-high heat in a deep heavy pot, large enough to hold the pineapple on its side. Add the brown sugar and vanilla bean. Cook, stirring,

to melt and caramelize the sugar, 3 to 5 minutes. Lay the pineapple in the pot and let it simmer, turning on all sides to brown. Add ½ cup water to the pan, reduce the heat to medium-low, cover, and cook, basting occasionally, until the pineapple is roasted through to the core, about 1 hour. If needed, add more water a tablespoon at a time. Let the pineapple cool in the pan, then lift it out, wrap it in plastic, and refrigerate it overnight. Reserve the pan juices.

Make the sherbet: Combine the sugar and 2 cups water in a saucepan and bring to a boil. Let the syrup cool slightly, then whisk in the buttermilk and lime juice. Refrigerate the mixture until cold, then freeze it in the ice-cream machine.

When ready to serve, assemble the dessert: Thinly slice the pineapple. If desired, rewarm the pan juices. Line 2 small scoops of sherbet down the center of the pineapple slices, then fold the sides up over the sherbet, as for a crepe. Arrange on serving plates and drizzle the pan juices on top. Serve immediately.

tasting trio

Myrna's Toasted Coconut–Chocolate Bars

Caramel–Orange Rice Crisps

Key Lime Sherbet

mini granita watermelons

MAKES 12

See photograph, page 163

I have a fatal weakness for cute desserts that are molded to look like other things, and I'm always on the lookout for new ones. (Once my friend Mary even made tiny sandwich cookies that looked just like hamburgers, with Nilla-wafer buns, fresh mint lettuce leaves, and chocolate patties.) One day in my pastry kitchen, I was stuffing scoops of bright pink granita into green cups of lime peel when I realized how much they looked like halves of tiny, real watermelons. But they were too smooth and clean. I sprinkled on a handful of currants to look like seeds, and after I stopped laughing this fetching dessert went on the menu.

Since watermelon contains so much water, the granita tastes best when you add sugar syrup and lime juice to intensify the flavor. You need to start this a day ahead.

6 limes
¼ cup sugar
4 cups watermelon pieces, seeds removed
⅛ teaspoon pure vanilla extract
40 currants

you'll need

2 empty ice-cube trays

Warm the limes in the microwave for 30 seconds to slightly soften them (this will make them easier to juice). Cut a thin slice off each end of the limes to make a flat base for each half to rest on. Cut the limes in half and squeeze out the juice into a medium bowl. Using a teaspoon or grapefruit spoon, scrape the remaining pulp and membranes out of the lime halves to make cups (discard the pulp). Transfer the cups to a plastic bag and refrigerate until ready to fill.

Combine ½ cup water with the sugar in a saucepan and bring to a boil. Set the syrup aside to cool.

Purée the watermelon cubes in a food processor or blender, then strain through a coarse strainer into the bowl containing the lime juice. Stir in the vanilla extract and cooled sugar syrup. Pour the mixture into the ice-cube trays and freeze overnight. *(The recipe can be made up to this point and kept frozen for up to 1 day.)*

When ready to serve, turn the watermelon ice cubes into a food processor fitted with a metal blade or into a powerful blender. Pulse the machine until the granita has the texture of crushed ice. Fill the lime halves very full with the granita, rounding the tops. Dot with the currants, making them look like watermelon seeds. Serve immediately.

tasting trio

Orange–Vanilla "Fried Eggs" on Cinnamon Toast

Meringue Cigarettes

Mini Granita Watermelons

nutmeg ice cream with gingerbread wafers

MAKES ABOUT 12 SERVINGS

There's something remarkably festive about this combination of creamy–spicy ice cream and crisp, toasty wafers. It's partly because the flavors will remind everyone of eggnog and gingersnaps—but it's also because you eat it just like chips and dip, scooping up the creamy with the crisp. The malt powder in the ice cream underlines the warm, toasty flavor of the nutmeg, but you can leave it out if you wish. The gingerbread recipe will yield a lot of crisps, so you may want to slice only half of it.

you'll need

- An ice-water bath (see page 21)
- A candy thermometer (optional)
- An ice-cream machine
- A baking pan, about 9 x 12 inches, lined with parchment or wax paper

FOR THE ICE CREAM

2 cups heavy cream
2 cups half-and-half
½ vanilla bean, split lengthwise
9 egg yolks
¾ cup sugar
Half of 1 whole nutmeg, grated
2 tablespoons malted milk powder (such as Carnation)

FOR THE GINGERBREAD

⅔ cup unsalted butter
1 cup (packed) light brown sugar
2 tablespoons molasses, light or dark (not blackstrap)
2 cups all-purpose flour
1 teaspoon baking powder
2 teaspoons baking soda
4 teaspoons ground ginger
⅔ cup milk
1 egg

Make the ice cream: Heat the cream, half-and-half, and vanilla bean in a saucepan over medium heat, stirring occasionally to make sure the mixture doesn't scorch on the bottom. When it reaches a fast simmer (do not let it boil), turn off the heat and set aside to infuse 10 to 15 minutes.

Whisk the egg yolks and sugar together. Whisking constantly, slowly pour the still-hot cream mixture into the egg yolk mixture. Return the mixture to the saucepan, place the thermometer, if using, in the mixture, and cook over medium heat, stirring constantly with a wooden spoon. At 160 degrees, the mixture will give off a puff of steam. When the mixture reaches 180 degrees, it will be thickened and creamy, like eggnog. If you're not using a thermometer, test it by dipping a wooden spoon into the mixture. Run your finger down the back of the spoon. If the stripe remains clear, the mixture is ready; if the edges blur, the mixture is not quite thick enough yet. When it is ready, quickly remove it from the heat.

Strain the mixture into a bowl to smooth it and remove the vanilla bean. Whisk in the grated nutmeg and the malt powder. Rest the bottom of the bowl in the ice bath and let the mixture cool, stirring often, about 2 hours. Freeze in the ice-cream machine.

Make the gingerbread: Heat the oven to 375 degrees.

Combine the butter, brown sugar, and molasses in a saucepan and melt over medium-high heat. Stir the dry ingredients together in a bowl. Pour in the butter mixture and mix to combine. Whisk the milk and egg together, then stir into the batter.

Pour the batter into the baking pan and bake until the gingerbread is firm, 40 to 45 minutes. Let the gingerbread cool, then chill it until cold (overnight, if possible).

recipe continues on next page

When ready to serve, heat the oven to 400 degrees. Using a serrated knife, slice the gingerbread ⅛ inch thick and arrange the slices on a cookie sheet. Toast until crisped. Serve with bowls of nutmeg ice cream.

tasting trio

Orange–Cardamom Chocolate Truffles

Chewy Butter Caramels

Nutmeg Ice Cream with Gingerbread Wafers

mini root beer floats

MAKES 8

This is so simple that it barely qualifies as a recipe, but you'd be surprised how people squeal with delight when you bring them to the table. I serve mine in small colored metallic cups that I picked up at a '50s theme store. Root beer is a surprisingly good complement to many other dessert flavors, including peanut, vanilla, lemon, butterscotch, and cinnamon.

you'll need

4 drinking straws, cut in half
A mini-ice-cream scoop or melon baller
8 small serving cups

3 cups root beer, well chilled
Vanilla ice cream

Rest half a drinking straw in each serving cup. Pour in root beer almost to the top. Use the scooper melon baller to place a round, tiny scoop of ice cream in each cup. Serve immediately.

root beer slush–vanilla cream cordial cups

MAKES 6 TO 8

This dessert may sound exotic, but it's really just a root beer float in reverse: The root beer is frozen and the ice cream is liquid. For the vanilla cream, you'll make ice cream up to the point of freezing—and then fold in soft whipped cream instead. The hot brew of cream, milk, egg yolks, sugar, and vanilla is also known as an *anglaise* sauce.

Cordial cups are like tiny wineglasses. People used to make "cordials," or liqueurs, from raspberries and other fruits; they were considered appropriate drinks for ladies.

Start this dessert one day in advance.

you'll need

- 1 or 2 ice-cube trays
- An ice-water bath (see page 21)
- 6 to 8 cordial or other small serving cups, preferably glass

1 cup root beer
¼ cup heavy cream
1 cup whole, 2% fat, or 1% fat milk
¼ vanilla bean, split lengthwise
3 egg yolks
⅓ cup sugar

The day before you plan to serve the dessert, pour the root beer into the ice-cube trays. Freeze overnight.

Also the day before, make the vanilla cream if you like: Whip the cream until stiff in a mixer fitted with a whisk attachment (or using a hand mixer). Refrigerate. Heat the milk and vanilla bean in a saucepan over medium heat, stirring occasionally to make sure the mixture doesn't scorch on the bottom. When it reaches a fast simmer (do not let it boil), turn off the heat and set the mixture aside to infuse for 10 minutes. In a medium bowl, whisk together the egg yolks and sugar. Whisking constantly, slowly pour the still-hot milk mixture into the egg yolk mixture. Return the mixture to the saucepan and cook over medium heat, stirring often, until the mixture is thick enough to coat the back of a spoon. Immediately remove from the heat. Pour the mixture through a fine sieve into a bowl and rest the bottom of the bowl in the ice bath. Let cool, stirring often. When the mixture is cold, fold in the whipped cream and keep it chilled overnight, until ready to serve.

When ready to serve, fill each serving cup halfway with the cream mixture. Turn the root-beer ice cubes into a food processor fitted with a metal blade or into a powerful blender. Pulse the machine until the root beer has the texture of crushed ice. Top the cream with spoonfuls of granita and serve immediately.

tasting trio

Chocolate Chipless Cookies

Orange–Vanilla "Fried Eggs" on Cinnamon Toast

Root Beer Slush—Vanilla Cream Cordial

Chocolate Doughnuts with Vanilla Malteds and Cranberry Jam

Indoor S'Mores

Black-and-White Chocolate Mousse Cups

Orange–Cardamom Chocolate Truffles

Hot Chocolate–Banana Wontons

Chocolate–Almond Fondue with Cake Cubes

Chocolate–Raspberry Pot Pies ◎ Chocolate Soufflé Pots

Hot Chocolate Turtle Soup

Chocolate Pots-de-Crème with Orange Whipped Cream

Fudge Tartlets with Peanut Butter Ice Cream and Cabernet

Caramel ◎ White-Hot Chocolate

Hot Cocoa Shots with Mini-Marshmallows

chocolate BITES

chocolate doughnuts with vanilla malteds and cranberry jam

MAKES 8 SERVINGS (ABOUT 30 DOUGHNUTS)

See photograph, page 167

These hot, moist dark chocolate bites are wonderful with a cold, creamy vanilla malted and a little dip of tangy jam. My friend Roy once shared with me a doughnut recipe that contained mashed potatoes, and I've never looked back. Later on, when I was doing a little research and development for the Krispy Kreme company, I learned that most commercial doughnuts have potato starch in their dough. It makes a softer, finer crumb than wheat flour, and helps keep the doughnut moist inside.

you'll need

- A doughnut cutter, 1½ inches in diameter, or a 1½-inch cookie cutter and a ½-inch cookie cutter
- A large cookie sheet, lined with parchment or wax paper or with nonstick baking mats (see page 16)
- A deep-frying thermometer
- A cookie sheet or tray, lined with paper towels
- 8 small decorative glasses, for serving the malteds
- 4 drinking straws, cut in half

FOR THE JAM

½ bag (6 ounces) cranberries, fresh or frozen
1 cup sugar

FOR THE DOUGHNUTS

½ ounce (2 envelopes) active dry yeast
¼ cup plus 2 tablespoons sugar
⅓ cup lukewarm water (about body temperature, 98.6 degrees F.)
¾ cup all-purpose flour
½ cup cake flour
¼ cup cocoa powder
¾ teaspoon baking soda
¼ cup hot water
3 ounces semisweet chocolate, melted (see page 11)
¼ cup confectioners' sugar
½ teaspoon salt
1 medium-large Idaho potato (about 6 ounces), boiled, peeled, and mashed or riced
Vegetable oil, for frying

FOR THE GLAZE

4 ounces semisweet chocolate, chopped
½ cup heavy cream

FOR THE MALTEDS

½ cup half-and-half
3 tablespoons malted milk powder (such as Carnation)
3 cups French vanilla ice cream

Make the jam: Combine 1 cup water with the cranberries and sugar in a saucepan and bring to a boil, stirring often. Cook until the cranberries pop, then continue cooking 1 minute more. Let the cranberries cool, then refrigerate until ready to serve.

Make the doughnuts: Combine the yeast, sugar, and lukewarm water in the bowl of a mixer, stirring until the yeast is dissolved. Add ¼ cup of the all-purpose flour and ¼ cup of the cake flour. Stir well and set aside to proof in a warm place until foamy, about 30 minutes.

Combine the cocoa powder and baking soda in a large bowl and add the hot water. Stir to dissolve. Add the melted chocolate to the cocoa powder mixture and mix. Add the confectioners' sugar, salt, and potato and mix.

Fit your mixer with the paddle attachment. Add the chocolate mixture, ¼ cup of the all-purpose flour, and the remaining ¼ cup of cake flour to the yeast mixture in the bowl and mix at low speed to combine. Mix at high speed for 30 seconds. Add the remaining ¼ cup of all-purpose flour and mix at high speed until combined. The dough may be sticky.

Flour a work surface heavily and knead the dough gently for about 30 sec-

recipe continues on next page

onds, just to bring it together. Transfer to a greased bowl and set aside to proof (rise) in a warm place until doubled in bulk, about 1½ hours. Punch the dough down, then proof another 30 minutes.

Flour a work surface heavily and pat the dough out to about ½ inch thick. Use the cutter to cut out doughnuts and then the holes, flouring the cutter each time. Set aside on the prepared cookie sheet.

Heat the oil in a deep-fryer (or 2 inches of oil in a deep, heavy pot fitted with the deep-frying thermometer) to 375 degrees. Line a cookie sheet with paper towels. Working in batches to avoid crowding the pan, and letting the oil return to 375 degrees between batches, slip the doughnuts into the oil. Flip once and cook no more than 30 seconds total (they burn easily). Set aside to drain and cool on the cookie sheet lined with paper towels. Cook the doughnut holes in the same manner, frying just 20 seconds and moving them around in the oil as they cook.

When the doughnuts have cooled, make the chocolate glaze: Place the chopped chocolate in a bowl. Bring the cream to a boil in a saucepan, pour it over the chocolate, and let it sit, whisking occasionally to melt the chocolate and combine the mixture. When the glaze is smooth, dip the doughnuts on one side in the warm glaze and set aside to cool.

Make the malteds: Combine the ingredients in a blender and blend until thick and creamy. Pour into serving glasses and place a half straw in each one.

Serve the doughnuts on plates with a dollop of jam on the side for dipping.

tasting trio

Caramel–
Orange Rice Crisps

Lemon Cream Daisies

Chocolate Doughnuts with
Vanilla Malteds and
Cranberry Jam

indoor s'mores

MAKES 16

When our restaurant Tru won its first four-star review, my partners and I thanked the staff with a "staff meal" of caviar, champagne, and foie gras. So when the second four-star review came in, we were stuck for a way to celebrate! We decided to go to the other extreme, with a feast of the best bratwurst (a Chicago classic), beer, and s'mores. I think we got even more respect for the second meal than we did for the first. It takes nerve for four-star chefs to serve s'mores!

My dear friend Karen reintroduced me to the molten, aromatic pleasures of this childhood treat. Just combine three bite-size ingredients—graham crackers, milk chocolate, and marshmallows—and apply heat. Add your own summer-camp memories and serve immediately.

32 miniature graham crackers
2 milk chocolate bars, the kind that can be broken into squares
8 marshmallows (or use ½ marshmallow recipe from Marshmallow Moons, page 40)

Heat the oven to 400 degrees.

Lay half of the graham crackers on a cookie sheet. Top with chocolate pieces to cover. Use a kitchen scissors to snip the marshmallows in half horizontally and place one half on top of each graham cracker.

Bake until the marshmallows are puffed and golden brown, 3 to 5 minutes. Remove from the oven and top with the remaining graham crackers, pressing down slightly to make a sandwich. Serve immediately, while still warm.

tasting trio

Mini Root Beer Floats

Raspberry Smallovers

Indoor S'Mores

black-and-white chocolate mousse cups

MAKES 10

In the '70s, when America was first discovering French cuisine, you couldn't go anywhere for dinner without having chocolate mousse for dessert. It was everywhere, and it was wonderful. In those carefree days, we knew nothing of cholesterol or salmonella, so mousses were made with whipped egg whites and raw yolks; now, mousses made with whipped cream have taken over. Whipped cream and chocolate make a very smooth, dense mousse. I add crème fraîche to my white chocolate mousse, to cut its sweetness.

Serve these dark and white mousses side by side in one cup, like the chocolate and vanilla ice-cream cups children eat with a wooden paddle. It's easy to do: Just cut a piece of smooth plastic (from the lid of a plastic tub or take-out container, for example) the same diameter as your ramekin. Stand it in the ramekin and pipe or spoon the mousses on either side, then slip the divider out carefully. The mousses are thick enough to stay separate.

To make the optional chocolate curls, buy milk chocolate (in a chunk), shave it into curls with a sturdy vegetable peeler, and don't worry if they break up into shards. Shards look nice, too.

you'll need

- 2 pastry bags fitted with large plain tips or 2 thick, resealable plastic bags (see page 15)
- A piece of flat, stiff plastic the same diameter as your ramekins (see above)
- 10 ramekins or 2½-inch metal collars (see page 19)

FOR THE DARK MOUSSE

6 ounces bittersweet chocolate
½ cup milk
1 cup heavy cream, whipped to soft peaks

FOR THE WHITE MOUSSE

6 ounces white chocolate
½ cup crème fraîche
1 cup heavy cream, whipped to soft peaks
Chocolate curls for serving (optional; see above)

Make the dark mousse: Melt the bittersweet chocolate (see page 11). Heat the milk in a saucepan until it is almost simmering and whisk it into the melted chocolate. Fold the whipped cream into the hot chocolate mixture; it will be rather soupy. Let the mixture cool slightly and transfer it to a pastry bag or resealable plastic bag. Refrigerate for at least 1 hour.

Make the white mousse: Melt the white chocolate (see page 11). Heat the crème fraîche in a saucepan until almost simmering and whisk it into the melted chocolate. Fold the whipped cream into the hot chocolate mixture; it will be rather soupy. Let the mixture cool slightly and transfer it to a pastry bag or resealable plastic bag. Refrigerate for at least 1 hour. *(The recipe can be made up to this point and kept refrigerated for up to 2 days.)*

If using collars, arrange them on a parchment paper–lined cookie sheet. Insert the plastic divider across the center of a collar or ramekin. If using plastic bags for piping, cut a corner off of each one. Pipe dark chocolate mousse on one side of the plastic, then white on the other. Pull out the plastic. Repeat with the rest of the mousse. Refrigerate until ready to serve.

When ready to serve, make the chocolate curls (see headnote). Remove the mousses from the refrigerator. If using collar molds, warm the metal with a hot, damp cloth and then lift off. Sprinkle the chocolate curls on top and serve.

tasting trio

Animal Crackers

Raspberry Smallovers

Black-and-White Chocolate Mousse Cups

orange–cardamom chocolate truffles

MAKES 50 TO 60

I sometimes wonder if there is any herb, spice, tea, nut, root, bark, infusion, or fruit that I *haven't* tried using to flavor chocolate truffles. Amazingly—and this proves just how delicious a well-made chocolate ganache is—there has only been one that didn't taste great. (So you won't be seeing a recipe for *herbes de Provence* truffles from me.)

This combination is one of the best, perfumed with sweet spice and citrus. Ganache is the simple blend of cream and chocolate that forms the silky center of the truffle. Since cream is naturally open to picking up other flavors, I always begin by infusing the flavorings in the cream or crème fraîche. Feel free to experiment with other seasonings, but always let the truffles come to room temperature before tasting so that the centers will soften and the flavors will blossom in your mouth.

Note that this recipe takes a couple of days to complete—but it can be completed up to a month in advance.

you'll need

- A pastry bag fitted with a large plain tip, optional (see page 15)
- A large cookie sheet, lined with parchment paper or with nonstick baking mats (see page 16); or a nonstick cookie sheet
- A large sheet pan with sides

1 orange
1½ cups crème fraîche
1 tablespoon cardamom pods, crushed
12 ounces best-quality bittersweet chocolate, chopped (see page 11)
24 ounces (1½ pounds) semisweet chocolate
1½ cups unsweetened Dutch-processed cocoa powder

Using a vegetable peeler, peel off the rind (orange part only) of the orange. Combine the crème fraîche, cardamom, and orange rind in a saucepan and bring to a boil over medium-high heat. As soon as it boils, turn off the heat and let the mixture infuse for 5 minutes.

Meanwhile, put the chopped bittersweet chocolate in a medium bowl. Strain the hot crème fraîche mixture over the chocolate. Whisk until the chocolate is melted and the mixture is smooth. Cover and let the mixture rest in a cool place (not the refrigerator; use a basement, porch, or other place where the temperature is about 55–60 degrees) overnight. The mixture will become firm but not stiff.

The next day, transfer the mixture to the pastry bag. Pipe bite-size "kisses" of the mixture onto the cookie sheet. Refrigerate briefly just until the truffles are set, about 30 minutes. Use your palm to gently tap down the point that sticks up on each truffle. Transfer to the freezer and freeze until hard, 2 to 3 hours; or cover with plastic and freeze overnight or up to 2 weeks.

Melt the semisweet chocolate in the top of a double boiler set over barely simmering water. Spread the cocoa powder out on the sheet pan with sides.

Working in 2 batches if necessary to avoid crowding the pan of cocoa, dip the frozen truffle centers one at a time into the melted chocolate. To dip the truffles, you can either use your hands (the melted chocolate won't be very hot) or drop them in, then lift them out with a fork, one at a time. Shake off any excess chocolate and set the truffle down in the cocoa. When the truffle centers are dipped and the chocolate has started to set, gently but thoroughly shake the sheet pan to roll the truffles around in the cocoa until coated. Carefully remove to another sheet pan and refrigerate, uncovered, for 30 minutes. (You can sift the unused cocoa and use it for another purpose.)

Transfer the truffles to an airtight container and keep them chilled until almost ready to serve. *(The recipe can be made up to this point and kept refrigerated for up to 1 month.)* Bring the truffles to room temperature before serving.

tasting trio

French Macaroons with Coffee Cream

Cannelés

Orange–Cardamon Chocolate Truffles

hot chocolate–banana wontons

MAKES 24

See photograph, page 165

Crisp little stuffed triangles, savory or sweet, are always irresistible to me. The filling for these is just a chunk of chocolate and a nugget of banana; they melt together during the cooking into a warm, oozy mouthful. A cool, fruity mango dipping sauce provides tangy contrast.

Premade wonton and eggroll wrappers make wonderful crusts for miniature pastries. They are very easy to work with and respond best to deep-frying, which turns them shatteringly crisp. You can find them frozen at many supermarkets and all Asian grocery stores. Wonton, not eggroll, wrappers are the right size and shape for this recipe; any brand will do.

you'll need

A deep-frying thermometer

FOR THE MANGO SAUCE (OPTIONAL)

1 ripe mango, peeled, seeded, and cut up
Freshly squeezed juice of 1 lime
1 tablespoon or more sugar
¼ cup pineapple juice

FOR THE WONTONS

8 ounces milk chocolate (chocolate bars are fine)
2 bananas, peeled and cut into 12 pieces each
24 wonton wrappers
Vegetable oil
Confectioners' sugar, for serving

Make the sauce: Combine all the ingredients in a blender or food processor and purée until smooth. Strain into a serving bowl. Taste for sweetness, adding more sugar a teaspoon at a time as needed. Refrigerate until ready to serve.

Make the wontons: Break or cut the milk chocolate into 24 reasonably equal pieces. Use your hands to smooth out and round off any jagged edges or sharp corners, so that they will not poke through the wonton skins.

Lay the wonton skins out on a work surface at an angle, so that they look diamond-shaped instead of square. Lay a slice of banana and a piece of chocolate in the lower half of each diamond. Paint around the edges of one wonton skin with water and fold the top point down to meet the bottom, forming a triangle. Gently press the edges together, trying to press out any air, and pinch the edges to seal. Place on a plate and repeat with the remaining ingredients. If not serving immediately, cover tightly with plastic wrap to prevent them from drying out. *(The recipe can be made up to this point and refrigerated for up to 10 hours.)*

When ready to serve, heat the oil in a deep-fryer or 2 inches of oil in a heavy saucepan to 365 degrees. Put a thick layer of paper towels next to the pot or on a sheet pan. Six at a time, drop the wontons in the oil and fry until golden brown, turning occasionally. Fish them out and drain on paper towels while you fry the rest. Sprinkle with confectioners' sugar and divide on serving plates. Serve with individual bowls of mango sauce for dipping.

chocolate–almond fondue with cake cubes

MAKES 4 SERVINGS

I love chocolate fondue, but I can never seem to find my fondue pot when I need it! So I devised a way to have fondue in a bowl—or even straight out of the saucepan. With my quick fondue, it's easy to curl up on the sofa and watch movies on a rainy Friday night.

If you're the kind of person who can't wait for the pudding to chill in the fridge, you'll love this hot chocolate "goop." I use squares of pound cake for dipping, because it is moist and won't fall apart in the bowl. Cheesecake, chilled and cubed, would also work.

¼ cup sugar
4 teaspoons cornstarch
2 cups milk
5 ounces semisweet chocolate, chopped (see page 11)
1 egg yolk
½ teaspoon pure vanilla extract
½ teaspoon pure almond extract
3 to 6 fresh strawberries per person, with green tops
1 pound cake (see page 98), baked, cooled, and cut into 1-inch cubes

Combine the sugar and cornstarch in a saucepan over medium-high heat. Slowly pour in the milk, whisking until combined and no lumps of cornstarch remain. Cook over medium heat, whisking, until the mixture boils and just begins to thicken. Add the chocolate and whisk until it melts. Pour a few tablespoons of the milk–chocolate mixture into the egg yolk and whisk to combine. Pour the egg yolk mixture back into the saucepan. Return to the stove, reduce the heat to medium, and cook, stirring constantly, until the fondue is smooth and thick, about 30 seconds.

Remove the fondue from the heat and stir in the extracts. Transfer to a serving bowl and serve with strawberries and pound cake chunks for dipping.

tasting trio

Peppermint Stick–White Chocolate Bark

Orange–Honey-Glazed Almonds

Chocolate–Almond Fondue

chocolate–raspberry pot pies

MAKES 10 TO 12; CAN BE HALVED

See photograph, page 169

You can stop flipping pages now: Here's the surest crowd-pleaser in the whole book. Like any pot pie, it's made up of a warm, creamy filling with a crisp top crust. My dessert version offers an oozy flourless chocolate cake center, with juicy raspberries suspended in the hot chocolate, and then a flaky dark-chocolate cookie crust on top.

My pastry sous-chef Megan Kehoe fine-tuned this recipe until it was absolutely perfect, with a wonderful balance of flavors and textures. We always serve the pies warm—and sometimes we can't resist eating them right out of the oven. But you can also let them cool, then reheat them in the oven or a microwave just before serving.

you'll need

10 to 12 ramekins (see page 19)

FOR THE CRUST

8 tablespoons (1 stick) cool unsalted butter, cut into pieces
⅜ cup sugar
1 egg yolk
¼ teaspoon pure vanilla extract
¼ teaspoon baking powder
Scant 1½ cups all-purpose flour
¼ teaspoon salt
¼ cup cocoa powder, plus extra for rolling

FOR THE FILLING

6 egg yolks
4 eggs
¼ cup sugar
18 ounces semisweet chocolate, melted (see page 11)
10 tablespoons (1 stick plus 2 tablespoons) unsalted butter, melted
1 cup raspberries
Whipped cream for serving (optional)

Make the crust: Cream the butter and sugar in a mixer fitted with a paddle attachment (or using a hand mixer) until fluffy. Add the egg yolk and vanilla and mix.

Stir the remaining crust ingredients together, then add to the butter mixture and mix. Form the dough into a disk, wrap in plastic wrap, and chill for 1 hour.

When the dough is chilled, sprinkle a work surface with cocoa. Roll the dough out to about ⅛ inch thick, then cut rounds to fit the tops of the pies. Cover the tops with plastic wrap and chill while they rest.

Heat the oven to 375 degrees.

Make the filling: Combine the egg yolks, the whole eggs, and the sugar in a mixer fitted with a whisk attachment and whip until fluffy and light. Stir the melted chocolate into the egg mixture. Stir in the melted butter.

Use a ladle or pitcher to divide the filling among the ramekins. Gently push 3 raspberries down into each one. Arrange the ramekins on a baking sheet and bake for 6 minutes. Remove the pies but leave the oven on.

Top each pie with a round of chocolate crust and bake for another 8 to 10 minutes, until crisp. Let the pies cool slightly and serve with whipped cream. Or let them cool completely and rewarm them before serving. Serve the same day.

tasting trio

Peanut Butter Cookie–Grape Jelly Ice Cream Sandwiches

Caramel–Orange Rice Crisps

Pot Pies

chocolate soufflé pots

MAKES 8 TO 10

See photograph, page 168

Light but marvelously rich, this dessert is the last word in pure chocolate pleasure. That's because there's nothing to distract you from the flavor; the texture is smooth and easy, like that of a slumped, dense, moist soufflé. You may never look at an egg the same way after making this recipe: Note that the ingredients list calls separately for egg yolks, egg whites, *and* a whole egg. The taste isn't eggy, but the yolks contribute richness and the whites, whipped stiff, are what make the soufflé airy and soft.

To make cocoa powder, the cocoa butter is removed from the ground roasted bean, leaving only a dry concentrate of chocolate. It produces a very intense chocolate flavor, and I add butter back into the mixture to restore the texture. Cocoa that has been "Dutched" has been processed to mellow out its natural acidity.

you'll need

A hot-water bath (see page 21)

8 to 10 ramekins (see page 19)

10 tablespoons (1 stick plus 2 tablespoons) unsalted butter, at room temperature
⅓ cup plus 6 tablespoons sugar, divided
1 tablespoon plus 1 teaspoon cocoa powder, preferably Dutch-processed
4 egg yolks
1 egg
6 ounces bittersweet chocolate, melted (see page 11)
1 cup egg whites (from about 7 eggs)
Whipped cream for serving (optional)

Cream the butter in a mixer fitted with a whisk attachment (or using a hand mixer) until soft and fluffy. Add the ⅓ cup of sugar and mix. With the mixer running at low speed, blend in the cocoa powder. Add the egg yolks and the whole egg, then drizzle in the melted chocolate and mix until smooth.

In a clean, dry bowl, whip the egg whites until soft peaks form, then gradually pour in the 6 tablespoons of sugar and continue whipping until glossy and stiff. Fold the egg whites into the chocolate mixture and let it rest for at least 30 minutes (this is to allow some air to escape). *(The recipe can be made up to this point and kept refrigerated for up to 2 days.)*

When ready to serve, heat the oven to 375 degrees. Prepare the hot-water bath. Pour the batter into the ramekins, filling each one three-fourths full, and bake just until set, 10 to 12 minutes. Serve the soufflé pots warm, in the cups. Top with a dollop of whipped cream if you like.

tasting trio

Elsie's Baby Rugelach

Green Grapes Glacé

Chocolate Soufflé Pots

hot chocolate turtle soup

MAKES
8 SERVINGS

To make this sundae-like dessert, I deconstructed the original chocolate turtle into chocolate, pecans, and caramel and then put it back together as rich hot cocoa, butter pecan ice cream, and caramel sauce. You make your own turtles, to swim around the side of the plate.

you'll need

A candy thermometer

A large cookie sheet, well greased or lined with parchment paper or with nonstick baking mats (see page 16); or a nonstick cookie sheet

FOR THE TURTLES

1 cup (packed) light brown sugar
1 cup granulated sugar
1 cup dark corn syrup
8 tablespoons (1 stick) unsalted butter
2 cups evaporated milk
1 teaspoon pure vanilla extract
3 cups pecan halves
8 ounces semisweet chocolate

FOR THE SOUP

8 ounces bittersweet chocolate, chopped (see page 11)
1½ cups half-and-half
12 coffee beans, crushed
½ cup light corn syrup
½ teaspoon pure vanilla extract

Milk for thinning the sauce, as needed
8 small scoops butter pecan ice cream

Make the turtles: Combine the sugars, corn syrup, butter, and 1 cup of the evaporated milk in a saucepan fitted with a candy thermometer and bring to a boil. Slowly add the remaining evaporated milk, stirring constantly, and cook until the mixture reaches 255 degrees. Ladle out ½ cup of the mixture and set it aside (you'll use this later as a caramel sauce). Add the vanilla and pecans to the pot and mix well.

Spoon the mixture in dollops onto the cookie sheet, trying to get 5 pecans in each one. If you like, adjust the pecans so that they stick out like the legs and head of a turtle. Don't spread them out too much; the pecans should be touching each other or the turtles will be too big. Refrigerate until set.

Once the turtles are firm, melt the semisweet chocolate (see page 000). Set a wire rack over a piece of parchment paper or paper towels. Drop the turtles into the chocolate one by one and fish them out gently with a fork. Place them on the wire rack and let the excess chocolate drip off for a bit. Return the turtles to the cookie sheet to set until firm. Store at room temperature in an airtight container until ready to serve. *(The recipe can be made up to this point and held for up to 5 days.)*

Make the soup: Put the chopped chocolate in a mixing bowl. Put the half-and-half and coffee beans in a saucepan and bring to a boil over medium-high heat. Pour the mixture over the chocolate and whisk until the mixture is smooth. Add the corn syrup and vanilla and whisk together. Pour the mixture through a strainer into a serving pitcher. If you're not serving immediately, chill until serving.

When ready to serve, heat the reserved ½ cup caramel sauce in the microwave, adding milk to thin it as needed. Heat the pitcher of chocolate soup in the microwave. Put a small scoop of butter pecan ice cream in each of 8 serving cups and drizzle with caramel sauce. At the table, pour the hot chocolate soup over the ice cream. Serve with turtles on the side.

tasting trio

Coconut–Pistachio Tuiles

Ruby Raspberry Jellies

Hot Chocolate Turtle Soup

chocolate pots-de-crème with orange whipped cream

MAKES 8 TO 10

See photograph, page 168

Truly the ultimate chocolate pudding. After the first bite, you may have to lie down on the sofa and have the rest fed to you from a silver spoon. It's that good—that smooth, that creamy, that chocolate-enriched—and it's not too sweet, which helps the chocolate flavor shine.

Here's the secret to the superiority of this pudding: There is no thickener other than egg yolks and cream (no cornstarch or gelatin, unlike our usual chocolate pudding recipes). It's the traditional formula for pots-de-crème, a favorite French childhood dessert.

you'll need

- 8 to 10 ramekins (see page 19)
- A hot-water bath (see page 21)

FOR THE CUSTARD

- 4 ounces best-quality bittersweet chocolate, chopped (see page 11)
- 4 cups heavy cream
- Pinch of salt
- 6 egg yolks
- ½ cup sugar

FOR THE WHIPPED CREAM

- ½ cup heavy cream, chilled
- ½ teaspoon sugar
- ¼ teaspoon freshly grated orange zest

Make the custard: Heat the oven to 300 degrees.

Place the chopped chocolate in a bowl. Combine the cream and salt in a saucepan and bring to a boil over medium-high heat. As soon as it boils, remove it from the heat and pour it over the chocolate, mixing until melted. Put the saucepan back on the stove.

Whisk the yolks and sugar together in a medium bowl. A little at a time, add all the hot chocolate mixture to the egg mixture, mixing after each addition. Pour the mixture back into the saucepan and heat it over medium heat until it is slightly thickened. The mixture should be thick enough to smoothly coat the back of a wooden spoon. Run your finger down the back of the spoon; when the edges do not blur, the mixture is ready.

Pour the mixture into the ramekins and place in the hot-water bath. Cover the pan tightly with foil and bake in the center of the oven until almost set but still jiggly in the center, 30 to 40 minutes. (The custards will finish cooking as they cool.) Remove from the water bath and let cool for 15 minutes. Tightly cover each ramekin with plastic wrap, making sure the plastic does not touch the surface of the custard. Refrigerate for at least 2 hours or until ready to serve.

Just before serving, whip the cream with the sugar and orange zest. Spoon a dollop onto each pot-de-crème.

tasting trio

Pecan Shortbread Bites

Hot Chocolate–Banana Wontons

Chocolate Pots-de-Crème

fudge tartlets with peanut butter ice cream and cabernet caramel

MAKES ABOUT 24; CAN BE HALVED

The elements of this dessert may sound exotic, but look closer: It's all strangely familiar. Chocolate fudge with salty peanut butter is snatched from a Reese's peanut-butter cup, and the combination of peanut butter and sweet grapes (caramel sauce infused with red wine) is lifted directly from a peanut butter and jelly sandwich. I love to take desserts apart and then put the pieces back together in a new, fresh way. This has been a signature dessert at Tru from Day One.

The caramel sauce is a beautiful garnet red, fruity and tangy in flavor from the wine (but with no alcohol taste). Chocolate fudge and peanut butter make a rich, unctuous combination; the sauce lightens the flavors and weaves them together. Finish baking the fudge tarts the same day you plan to serve them.

you'll need

- An ice-water bath (see page 21)
- An ice-cream machine
- At least 2 mini-muffin tins, 24 cups each
- Nonstick cooking spray

FOR THE ICE CREAM

- 1 quart (4 cups) half-and-half
- ½ vanilla bean, split lengthwise
- 9 egg yolks
- ¾ cup sugar
- ⅜ cup peanut butter, preferably smooth

FOR THE CRUSTS

- 2 cups all-purpose flour
- ½ cup sugar
- 8 tablespoons (1 stick) cold unsalted butter, cut into small pieces
- 2 egg yolks
- 1 tablespoon heavy cream
- ¼ teaspoon pure vanilla extract

FOR THE FILLING

7 ounces bittersweet chocolate
2 tablespoons unsalted butter
7 eggs
½ cup sugar
¾ teaspoon pure vanilla extract
½ teaspoon salt

FOR THE SAUCE

4 cups sugar
1½ cups red wine, Cabernet or another full-bodied wine

Make the ice cream: Heat the half-and-half and vanilla bean in a saucepan over medium heat, stirring occasionally to make sure the mixture doesn't scorch on the bottom. When the cream mixture reaches a fast simmer (do not let it boil), turn off the heat. Set the mixture aside to infuse for 10 to 15 minutes.

Whisk together the egg yolks and sugar in a medium bowl. Whisking constantly, slowly pour the hot half-and-half mixture into the egg yolk mixture. Return the mixture to the saucepan and cook over medium heat, stirring constantly with a wooden spoon. At 160 degrees, the mixture will give off a puff of steam. When the mixture reaches 180 degrees, it will be thickened and creamy, like eggnog. Test it by dipping a wooden spoon into the mixture. Run your finger down the back of the spoon. If the stripe remains clear, the mixture is ready; if the edges blur, the mixture is not quite thick enough yet. When it is ready, quickly remove it from the heat.

Immediately whisk in the peanut butter and whisk until smooth. Strain

recipe continues on next page

the mixture into a bowl to smooth it and remove the vanilla bean. Rest the bottom of the bowl in the ice bath and let the mixture cool, stirring often, for 2 hours. Freeze according to the directions of the ice-cream machine.

Make the crusts: In a mixer fitted with a paddle attachment (or using a hand mixer), mix the flour and sugar. Add the butter and mix until coarse and sandy.

Whisk the egg yolks, cream, and vanilla together. Add to the flour mixture and mix at low speed just until combined. If the mixture seems too dry, add another teaspoon of heavy cream. Turn the dough out onto a work surface and form into a disk. Wrap in plastic wrap and refrigerate for at least 1 hour, until ready to use. *(The recipe can be made up to this point and kept refrigerated for up to 2 days.)*

Roll out the dough ⅛ inch thick on a lightly floured surface and cut out circles that are 2 inches larger in diameter than the mini-muffin cups.

Spray the muffin tin well with nonstick cooking spray, then gently press the dough rounds into the cups, easing the dough completely into the cups. Smooth out the folds by pressing the dough against the sides and bottoms of the cups (the walls will become a little thicker). Use your fingers to form the rim of each tartlet into an even edge, pulling or cutting off extra bits of dough if necessary.

Spray the bottom of another mini-muffin tin with nonstick spray and gently push it down into the tin with the dough rounds so that it "spoons" into the bottom cups. This will help prevent shrinkage during baking. Chill for 30 minutes.

Heat the oven to 375 degrees. Keeping the tins pressed together, turn them upside down on a sheet pan. Bake until the crusts are dry and golden but not brown, about 12 minutes. Let them cool upside down for 20 minutes, then invert the pans and carefully lift the top tin out, leaving the pastry cups in the bottom tin.

Meanwhile, make the filling: Melt the chocolate and butter together in the top of a double boiler set over barely simmering water, stirring frequently. When melted, remove the mixture from the heat and whisk in the eggs, sugar, vanilla, and salt.

Heat the oven to 350 degrees. Pour the filling into the prebaked tart shells (still in their tins) and bake for 11 to 13 minutes, until the filling is set at the edges but still a little moist in the center.

Meanwhile, make the caramel sauce: Pour the sugar into the center of a deep saucepan. Carefully pour ½ cup water around the sugar, trying not to splash any sugar onto the sides of the pan. Do not stir; gently draw your finger through the center of the sugar to moisten it. Over high heat, bring the mixture to a full boil and cook without stirring, swirling the pot occasionally to even out the color, until it is amber-caramel, 10 to 20 minutes. When the mixture is done, immediately remove the pot from the heat. Use a wooden spoon to slowly stir in the red wine. Set aside.

When ready to serve, arrange the tarts on serving plates. Put a dollop of the sauce on the plate on one side of the tart and a small scoop of the ice cream on the other side. Serve immediately.

tasting trio

White-Hot Chocolate

Jelly Doughnut Holes

Fudge Tartlets with Peanut Butter Ice Cream and Cabernet Caramel

white-hot chocolate

This rich and fragrant brew is scented with vanilla and star anise. It makes an elegant, warming dessert drink that looks beautiful in your best china teacups.

MAKES 2 CUPS

See photograph, page 166

4 ounces white chocolate, chopped
½ teaspoon pure vanilla extract
1¾ cups milk
¼ cup heavy cream
3 pieces of star anise

Combine the chopped chocolate and vanilla extract in a medium bowl. Combine the milk, cream, and star anise in a saucepan and heat over medium-high heat until boiling, stirring occasionally. Pour the milk mixture over the chocolate and whisk well to melt. Strain the beverage into mugs to smooth it and to remove the star anise (or just fish them out), and serve immediately.

hot cocoa shots with mini-marshmallows

MAKES 4 CUPS

See photograph, page 166

It's fun to sip these tiny cups of dark, cinnamony hot chocolate. They are great with cookies, and with almost any other dessert you can think of! And you should encourage guests to sip through the cinnamon stick—just like a straw.

4 cups whole milk
¼ teaspoon pure vanilla extract
¼ cup cocoa powder
½ cup sugar
¼ teaspoon cinnamon
½ recipe marshmallow (from Marshmallow Moons, page 40) placed in a pastry bag fitted with a small plain tip, or mini-marshmallows, for serving
Cinnamon sticks, for garnish (optional)

Place the milk in a saucepan and heat to a simmer over medium heat.

Meanwhile, stir together the cocoa powder, sugar, and cinnamon. A few teaspoons at a time, stir some of the hot milk into the cocoa mixture to make a smooth paste. Scrape the cocoa mixture into the saucepan with the remaining milk and simmer for 2 minutes; do not let it boil. Turn off the heat and add the vanilla.

Pour the cocoa into small serving cups and pipe or place 4 mini-marshmallows in each cup. Add a cinnamon stick, if using. Serve immediately.

Raspberry Smallovers ◎ Red, White, and Blueberry Salad

Real Fruit Cocktail ◎ Green Grapes Glacé

Striped Juice Shots ◎ Fairground Apple Fritters

Lemon Meringue Beehives ◎ Passionate Raspberry Gratins

Watermelon Cubes with a Kiwi–Lime Shot

Roasted Plums on the Half Shell with Fromage Blanc

Roasted Strawberries with Cherry Balsamic Sauce

Gio's Silver-Dollar Apple Pancakes with Maple Beurre Blanc

Taffy Lady Apples ◎ Pineapple and Melon Ball Brochettes

Jelly Doughnut Holes

Tiny Honey Biscuits with Crème Fraîche and Berries

Cranberry and Cream Jelly Hearts

Fannie's Banana–Blueberry–Sour Cream Salad

Petit Popovers with Peach Butter ◎ Apricot Tartes Tatin

Little Apple Brown Betties ◎ Clementines in Mint Syrup

Sugar-Frosted Frozen Grapes

Vanilla-Crusted Strawberries

Vacherins with Raspberries and Cream

fruity BITES

raspberry smallovers

MAKES 12

Every family has its legends, and in mine there is none more hotly contested than The Day Dad Ate My Danish. From a young age, I was addicted to the raspberry cheese danishes at our local bakery, a sublime concoction of flaky pastry, lemon-scented pot cheese, and raspberry preserves. I saved up and bought one on a Saturday, then squirreled it away in the refrigerator to savor later. . . . Well, you can imagine the rest. We still can't agree on whether that danish was fair game!

Now, of course, it doesn't matter, because I can make these easy and shockingly delicious tiny turnovers anytime I want. I even share them with my wonderful dad.

you'll need

A large cookie sheet, well greased or lined with parchment paper or with nonstick baking mats (see page 16); or a nonstick cookie sheet

2 sheets of frozen puff pastry, thawed
4 ounces cream cheese
1 egg yolk
¼ cup confectioners' sugar
½ teaspoon pure vanilla extract
½ teaspoon freshly grated lemon zest
1 cup raspberries
1 egg, beaten with 2 teaspoons water
2 tablespoons granulated sugar

Lightly flour a work surface. Roll out each sheet of puff pastry into a 9 × 12-inch rectangle; the pastry will become slightly thinner. Cover the sheets with plastic wrap and chill.

Mix the cream cheese, egg yolk, confectioners' sugar, vanilla, and lemon zest until smooth in a mixer fitted with a paddle attachment.

Using a sharp knife, cut the puff pastry into 3-inch squares.

Heat the oven to 375 degrees.

Lay a pastry square on a work surface and brush the edges with egg wash. In the center of the square, place 1 tablespoon of cheese filling. Place

3 raspberries on top. Brush the edges of a second pastry square with egg wash and place it on top of the filling (egg wash side down). Carefully press the edges together to seal them well. Transfer to the prepared cookie sheet and keep refrigerated. Repeat with the remaining ingredients, placing the smallovers 1 inch apart.

When the smallovers are all made, brush the tops with the egg wash and sprinkle with granulated sugar. Bake until they are golden brown, 20 to 25 minutes. Serve the smallovers warm or let them cool to room temperature. Serve within 1 day.

tasting trio

Chocolate Doughnuts with Vanilla Malteds and Cranberry Jam

Coffee Suckers on Cinnamon Sticks

Smallovers

red, white, and blueberry salad

MAKES 6 CUPS

Coconut milk and fresh mint give this red, white, and blue fruit salad a whiff of the breezy and the exotic. I do like to make this for Fourth of July parties. (I know it's corny, but what else are parties for?) But it is good throughout the summer, and white peaches and watermelon make a wonderfully fragrant combination. Try to use big, sweet blueberries. You can substitute apples for the white peaches, but if you do, serve the salad right away.

Serve the salad in red, white, and blue paper cups, or string the fruit on skewers in red, white, and blue stripes.

2 cups watermelon cubes
2 white peaches, pitted and cut into bite-size pieces
2 cups blueberries
2 tablespoons freshly squeezed lemon juice, or to taste
2 tablespoons sugar, or to taste
½ cup canned coconut milk
3 fresh mint leaves, julienned

Combine the fruits in a bowl. Whisk together the lemon juice, sugar, and coconut milk in a small bowl. Toss the dressing with the fruit and the mint. Taste for sugar and lemon juice and chill until ready to serve, up to 10 hours.

tasting trio

Patriotic Popcorn Balls

Indoor S'Mores

Red, White, and Blueberry Salad

real fruit cocktail

MAKES ABOUT 6 CUPS

Like most children of nutrition-conscious parents, I was completely fascinated as a kid by synthetic treats like Twinkies, Kool-Aid, and Tang. I was especially intrigued by the soft texture and tangy syrup of canned fruit cocktail, with those wonderful smooth green grapes; chunks of peach, pineapple, and pear; and a lone maraschino cherry. It was completely unlike the "real" fruit I was used to biting into!

This fresh version, bathed in citrus–vanilla syrup, is a wonderful fruit salad—and it only looks like the canned version. Maraschino cherries have been rehabilitated with the removal of dangerous red dyes from the market. Put in as many as you like, and don't forget to use extra grapes. Peel them if you like.

3 peaches, pitted and peeled
1 small bunch of green grapes
½ pineapple, peeled and cored
3 pears, peeled and cored
A few maraschino cherries or strawberries
1 cup blueberries (optional)
½ cup pineapple juice
½ cup fresh orange juice
2 tablespoons fresh lime juice, or to taste
2 tablespoons sugar, or to taste
¼ teaspoon pure vanilla extract

Cut up all the fruits into bite-size pieces and combine in a large bowl. In a small bowl, whisk together the remaining ingredients. Pour the dressing over the fruit and gently toss to coat. Chill the salad until ready to serve. Taste for sugar and lime juice and serve in small glasses.

tasting trio

Stained-Glass Cookies

Cherry Charlottes

Real Fruit Cocktail

green grapes glacé

MAKES 40

With a bunch of grapes in the fridge and sugar in the pantry, you can have grapes wearing chic caramel boots on the table in an hour—and most of that time is just for setting the caramel. Other fresh fruits, like fat berries or tangerine segments, can be caramelized in the same way. They must be served within about 2 hours of making, because the caramel will start to melt.

you'll need

- 40 toothpicks
- An ice-water bath (see page 21)
- A large cookie sheet, oiled or lined with a nonstick baking mat (see page 16)

40 large green grapes
1¼ cups sugar

Stick a toothpick into the bottom (not the stem end) of each grape.

Make the caramel: Pour the sugar into the center of a deep saucepan. Carefully pour ⅓ cup water around the walls of the pan, trying not to splash any sugar onto the walls. Do not stir; gently draw your finger twice through the center of the sugar, making a cross, to moisten it. Over high heat, bring to a full boil and cook without stirring, swirling the mixture in the pot occasionally to even out the color, until it is a light golden caramel, 4 to 8 minutes. When the caramel is cooked, dip the bottom of the pan in the ice bath for 15 seconds to stop the cooking.

Holding them by the toothpicks, dip the top of each grape into the caramel and set caramel side down on the cookie sheet. If the caramel isn't thick enough to hold up the grape, wait a minute and try again.

Let the grapes cool until the caramel is set, about 10 minutes. Serve within 2 hours.

tasting trio

Tomme de Savoie on Crispy Oat Rounds

The Best Cheese Crackers with Walnut-Stuffed Figs

Green Grapes Glacé

striped juice shots

MAKES 8 TO 10

See photograph, page 171

I've been preoccupied with Jell-O for as long as I can recall—since long before I became a pastry chef. As an art student, I remember making a bathtub full of Jell-0 as part of a commentary on women's creative lives. It's probably a good thing I became a pastry chef instead.

These days, I make my own light, fresh fruit gels from scratch, using real juices and powdered gelatin. It's a snap. I often serve them as a little teaser, or *amuse-bouche,* before dessert, or alone with a blob of cream. These striped cups are fun and tasty for adults, and of course they're perfect for children's parties. If you're really feeling childish, you can mix gummy worms into the middle layer: Princess Diana's butler, Paul Burrell, told me he used to do that for Prince Harry and Prince William on their birthdays.

you'll need

8 to 10 small clear glasses, about 4 ounces (½ cup) each

- 3 tablespoons powdered gelatin
- 1¼ cups strawberry–banana juice, or another pink or red fruit juice of your choice
- 1¼ cups purple grape juice
- 1¼ cups orange or tangerine juice

Sprinkle 1 tablespoon of the gelatin over the strawberry–banana juice in a small bowl and set aside for 5 minutes. Warm in the microwave for 30 seconds or on the stove to dissolve the gelatin, and strain the mixture into a small pitcher. Divide among the serving glasses and chill until set, about 30 minutes.

Repeat the process with the purple grape juice, pouring it on top of the strawberry–banana jelly, and chill to set. Repeat the process with the orange juice, chill to set, and serve cold.

tasting trio

Thimble Cookies

Butterfly Cupcakes

Striped Juice Shots

fairground apple fritters

MAKES 24

I've always tried to re-create the apple fritters I tasted at a medieval fair when I was a child. (We were a family of folksingers, so we attended a lot of fairs.) I clearly recall the crisp crust and buttery inside, but I also have a hazy memory of buckets of apples flying up and down on pulleys and a crew of peelers, plus a big cast-iron frying kettle. The fritters were so good mostly because they were so fresh, and that is certainly true in any century.

The usual firm, tart apple varieties, such as Granny Smiths, Ida Reds, or Cortlands, are good here. But if you can get your hands on heirloom varieties, from Braeburn to Northern Spy to the magnificently named Esopus Spitzenburg, this is a simple way to show off their distinctive flavors.

1¼ cups all-purpose flour
¾ cup apple cider
2 eggs, separated
1 tablespoon vegetable oil
⅛ teaspoon salt
4 apples
Vegetable oil for frying
2 tablespoons granulated sugar
Confectioners' sugar or cinnamon sugar, for sprinkling

you'll need
A deep-frying thermometer

Put the flour in a bowl and make a well in the center. Pour the cider, egg yolks, vegetable oil, and salt in the well and gently whisk the wet ingredients together. Whisking, gradually draw the flour into the wet ingredients, expanding the well as you go until you have a smooth batter. When it is smooth, set it aside for 20 minutes.

Peel and core the apples. Cut each apple into 6 wedges.

Heat the vegetable oil in a deep-fryer or 2 inches of oil in a deep, heavy pot to 350 degrees.

When ready to cook the fritters, whip the egg whites in a mixer fitted with a whisk attachment until soft peaks form. With the mixer running, drizzle in the granulated sugar and continue whipping just until the whites are stiff and glossy. Fold the whites into the batter until completely blended.

Working in batches to avoid crowding the pot, spear an apple wedge on a long fork and dip it into the batter. Drop into the oil and fry until golden brown, turning once. Drain the fritters on paper towels, sprinkle with confectioners' sugar or cinnamon sugar, and serve immediately.

tasting trio

Lemon Meringue Beehives

Gougères with Plum Jam

Fairground Apple Fritters

lemon meringue beehives

MAKES 20 TO 24

See photograph, page 170

Thick, tangy lemon curd, tender meringue, and crumbly pastry are clearly made for each other. I have been tinkering with the basic elements of lemon meringue pie for years, and however I put it back together, it's always great. These individual mounds look incredibly cute and are shockingly easy to do.

Toasting the meringue at the end, a touch borrowed from Baked Alaska, gives the dessert a caramelized, toasted-marshmallow flavor element.

you'll need

- A 2-inch cookie cutter
- A large cookie sheet, well greased or lined with parchment paper or with nonstick baking mats (see page 16); or a nonstick cookie sheet
- A small ice cream scoop or melon baller, about 1½ inches across
- A pastry bag fitted with a small plain tip (¼-inch or less)
- A kitchen torch (optional)

FOR THE PASTRY BASES

4 tablespoons cold unsalted butter, cut into pieces
1 cup all-purpose flour
¼ teaspoon salt
1 egg yolk
¼ cup crème fraîche

FOR THE LEMON CURD

3 eggs
¾ cup sugar
Freshly grated zest of 1½ lemons
½ cup fresh lemon juice (from about 3 lemons)
6 tablespoons cold unsalted butter

FOR THE MERINGUE

½ cup egg whites (from about 4 eggs)
½ cup sugar

Make the pastry bases: Mix the butter, flour, and salt in a mixer fitted with a paddle attachment until sandy. In a separate bowl, blend the egg yolk and crème fraîche. Add to the flour mixture and mix until barely combined. Form the dough into a disk, wrap it in plastic wrap, and refrigerate it for at least 2 hours or up to 3 days.

Make the lemon curd: Bring 2 inches of water to a simmer in a saucepan. Whip the eggs and sugar in a mixer fitted with a whisk attachment until light and fluffy. Add the lemon zest and juice and place the bowl over the simmering water (without letting the bowl touch the water; pour some water out if needed). Cook until the curd is thickened, whisking occasionally. Remove it from the heat and whisk in the butter. Let the curd cool to room temperature, cover, and freeze overnight or up to 3 days.

Bake the pastry bases: Heat the oven to 375 degrees. Flour a work surface. Roll out the dough to ⅛ inch thick and cut out 2-inch rounds. Transfer the rounds to the cookie sheet and prick them all over with a fork. Bake until they are light golden brown, 12 to 15 minutes. Let cool. *(The whole recipe can be made up to this point up to 3 days in advance.)*

Up to 6 hours before serving, assemble the dessert: Arrange the pastry bases in a pan that will fit in your freezer (use two if needed). Use the small ice-cream scoop to place a ball of frozen lemon curd (it won't be frozen solid) onto each round. Freeze until needed.

Whip the egg whites until foamy, then add the sugar and continue whipping until stiff and glossy. Transfer to the pastry bag. Pipe meringue around the base of each pastry round, spiraling around and up the lemon-curd dome and gradually enclosing the top to create a beehive (see photo). Heat the broiler to very hot (or fire up your kitchen torch) and broil until the meringue is lightly browned all over. Return to the freezer until ready to serve, up to 6 hours.

tasting trio

Blackberry Brown-Butter Financiers

Peppermint Stick–White Chocolate Bark

Lemon Meringue Beehives

passionate raspberry gratins

MAKES 8

Fresh raspberries slathered with an easy passionfruit *sabayon,* then broiled just until puffed and brown: Like many raspberry desserts, this is easy, elegant, and fast. You make it right on the plates. The *sabayon*—the French word for zabaglione, a light Italian custard sauce—is cooked before it goes onto the berries, so the broiling is just to heat the dessert through, puff the eggs, caramelize the sugars, and barely cook those juicy-sweet berries.

Bowls or ramekins could be used for this, but shallow plates will give you the highest proportion of delicious browned crust.

you'll need

8 ovenproof serving dishes (see headnote)

4 egg yolks
⅓ cup plus 2 tablespoons sugar
½ vanilla bean, split lengthwise
¼ cup passion-fruit, mango, or peach juice
¼ cup champagne
2 egg whites
2 cups (1 pint) raspberries

Bring 2 inches of water to a simmer in a saucepan. Whisk together the yolks, ⅓ cup sugar, and vanilla bean in a metal bowl (small enough to rest inside the top of the saucepan) until light and fluffy. Gradually whisk in the passion-fruit juice and champagne. Place the bowl over the simmering water (without letting the bowl touch the water; pour some out if needed) and cook, whisking constantly, until the mixture is light, fluffy, and thickened, 5 to 10 minutes. Remove the bowl from the heat and let the mixture cool slightly.

Whip the egg whites in a mixer until stiff but not dry. Add the remaining 2 tablespoons of sugar and continue whipping until the whites are glossy, about 30 seconds more. Fold into the warm egg yolk mixture, let the sabayon cool, and refrigerate it until ready to use.

When ready to serve, heat the broiler to high (don't use a kitchen torch for this). Divide the raspberries among the serving dishes and arrange the dishes on a cookie sheet. Spoon the sabayon on top of the berries, covering them completely. Broil until the tops are lightly browned and slightly puffed, 2 to 3 minutes. You may need to rearrange the plates halfway through the broiling to make sure the gratins brown evenly. Serve immediately.

tasting trio

Coconut–Pistachio Tuiles

Vanilla Snow with Maple Syrup

Passionate Raspberry Gratins

watermelon cubes with a kiwi-lime shot

MAKES 15 TO 20

Just a few grains of coarse salt bring out the flavor of watermelon. If you are a fan of watermelon margaritas, try adding tequila to the fruit purée.

Half of a medium-size watermelon
2 kiwi fruits
2 limes
¼ cup sugar
Coarse sea salt, or *fleur de sel* for serving

you'll need

A small melon baller

Peel the watermelon with a large, heavy knife. Cut the flesh into slabs about 1½ inches thick. Avoiding the seediest sections of the watermelon, cut the flesh into 1½-inch cubes. Use the small melon baller or measuring spoon to hollow out a depression in the top of each cube, forming a little cup to hold the kiwi-lime shot. Place the cubes on a serving platter and chill.

Make the kiwi-lime shots: Peel and roughly cut up the kiwis. Place the pieces in a blender or food processor, squeeze in the juice of the limes, and add the sugar. Pulse briefly just until smooth (overprocessing will pulverize the kiwi seeds and the mixture will turn gray), then strain the purée into a pitcher to remove the seeds. Add just a few seeds back into the purée, to signal that it's made from kiwi.

At the last moment, pour or spoon the purée into the depressions. Sprinkle very lightly with coarse salt. Eat with your fingers.

tasting trio

Lemon Cream Daisies

Pecan-Crusted Goat Cheese with Quince Compote

Watermelon Cubes

roasted plums on the half shell with fromage blanc

MAKES 12

Use dark-skinned plums for this when possible; the thicker skin helps to hold the shape. *Fromage blanc* is a fresh French cheese that is lower in fat than cream cheese but very creamy and mild. If you can't find it, use whole-milk ricotta or Italian mascarpone.

you'll need

A baking dish, about 9 inches square

2 tablespoons unsalted butter, melted
1 vanilla bean, split lengthwise
6 plums, any kind, halved lengthwise and pitted
2 tablespoons sugar
½ cup fromage blanc or another fresh soft cheese such as mascarpone
2 tablespoons honey
Cinnamon sugar for sprinkling (optional)

Heat the oven to 400 degrees. Pour the melted butter into the baking dish.

With the tip of a sharp knife, scrape the insides of the vanilla bean into the pan, reserving the outside pod. Place the plums cut side down in the pan. Sprinkle with the sugar and lay the vanilla pod on top of the plums. Bake until the plums are slightly slumped and feel a little soft, 10 to 12 minutes. Let cool in the pan to room temperature, then remove the plums from the pan and chill until ready to serve.

Meanwhile, combine the fromage blanc with the honey in a bowl and blend with a fork until smooth. Chill until ready to serve.

To serve, turn the plums over and spoon the cheese filling into the cavity. Sprinkle with cinnamon sugar (if using) and serve immediately.

tasting trio

Elsie's Baby Rugelach

Sour Cream Seed Cakes with Earl Grey Glaze

Roasted Plums on the Half Shell

roasted strawberries with cherry balsamic sauce

MAKES 28

Ripe strawberries sprinkled with a few drops of rich, salty–sweet balsamic vinegar is an classic Italian summer dessert. But the combination requires perfectly ripe strawberries and flawlessly aged balsamic—hard things for ordinary mortals to get on an ordinary day. So here's my realists' rendition. Cherry balsamic vinegar is a wonderful flavoring, but good-quality plain balsamic will work too.

I roast the strawberries with vanilla, butter, and sugar to tenderize and sweeten them, then borrow a technique from the savory side of the kitchen by simmering the pan juices with wine and vinegar. I drop each strawberry onto a crisp butter-cookie base, then whisk a little butter into the sauce and drizzle that on top. The result is fragrant, fruity, rich, and light all at once.

4 tablespoons unsalted butter, melted
1 vanilla bean, split lengthwise
28 strawberries, tops cut off
2 tablespoons light brown sugar
2 tablespoons cherry or plain balsamic vinegar (see Sources, page 300)
3 tablespoons red wine
1 tablespoon cold unsalted butter, cut into small pieces
1 recipe Thimble Cookies (page 48), cut out with a 1-inch cookie cutter and omitting the final sprinkling of sugar, or 28 good-quality butter cookies of your choice

you'll need

A baking dish, about 9 inches square

Heat the oven to 400 degrees. Pour the melted butter into the baking dish (or melt it right in the dish).

Use the tip of a sharp knife to scrape the insides of the vanilla bean into the dish. Place the strawberries (cut side down) in the dish. Sprinkle the berries with the brown sugar and lay the vanilla pod over the berries. Bake until the berries are slumped and feel soft, 10 to 12 minutes. Let cool 20 minutes, then remove the berries from the pan and scrape the pan juices into a small skillet.

Add the balsamic vinegar and red wine to the skillet and heat the mixture to a simmer. Turn off the heat and whisk in the cold butter. Keep barely warm and use within an hour to retain the buttery smoothness. (If the sauce becomes too hot, the butter will separate. If this happens, try whizzing the sauce with an immersion blender or in a blender.)

When ready to serve, place each strawberry on a butter cookie. Divide among serving plates. Drizzle the warm sauce over and serve immediately.

tasting trio

Bread Puddings with Orange Marmalade

Mint–Chocolate-Chip Meringues

Strawberries

gio's silver-dollar apple pancakes with maple beurre blanc

MAKES 12

Silver-dollar pancakes were the first miniature food I encountered as a child, and I have been enchanted by them ever since. You get so many! My son, Gio, who mastered our Sunday-morning pancake ritual at age three, feels the same way. We both like these for dessert, too. They are rather like a miniature apple *clafoutis,* the French country classic. Beurre blanc is also a French classic, an emulsion of butter in liquid (usually white wine). I use maple syrup as the liquid, then whisk in the butter to create a thick sauce that is butter and syrup in one!

FOR THE SAUCE

½ cup maple syrup
⅓ cup water
⅓ cup (packed) light brown sugar
Freshly grated zest of ½ orange
½ vanilla bean, split lengthwise
1 cinnamon stick, 2 to 3 inches long
6 tablespoons cold unsalted butter, cut into pieces

FOR THE PANCAKES

1 cup all-purpose flour
1 teaspoon baking soda
½ teaspoon salt
1 tablespoon light brown sugar
2 eggs
1 cup plain yogurt
2 tablespoons unsalted butter, melted
Butter for cooking
2 tart, firm apples, peeled, cored, and sliced ¼ inch thick

Make the sauce: Combine all the ingredients except the butter in a saucepan and bring to a simmer. Turn off the heat and let the mixture sit for 10 minutes to infuse the flavors. Without turning the heat back on, whisk in the butter one piece at a time to thicken the sauce. Strain out the flavorings and keep the sauce warm in a pan of hot water or on a flame tamer on your stovetop. (If the sauce becomes too hot, the emulsification may "break" and the butter will separate. If this happens, try whizzing the sauce with an immersion blender or in a blender.)

Make the pancakes: Put a serving platter to heat in a 225-degree oven.

Combine the flour, baking soda, salt, and brown sugar in a large bowl and stir together. Whisk the eggs and yogurt together in a small bowl. Stir the egg mixture into the dry ingredients until almost smooth (leave some lumps; do not overmix), then stir in the melted butter.

Melt a few teaspoons of butter in a large skillet and sauté the apple slices just until tender. Remove half of the apples from the pan and set aside. Divide the apples in the pan into little piles of 2 or 3 slices and flatten slightly. Turn the heat to medium and pour or ladle a few tablespoons of batter over each apple pile to make a small pancake. Cook on one side until golden brown, then flip to cook the other side. Remove to the warm platter, return to the oven, and repeat with the remaining apples and batter. Serve with warm maple beurre blanc.

tasting trio

Blue Cheese Fritters with Pear Salad

Caramel–Orange Rice Crisps

Apple Pancakes

taffy lady apples

MAKES 12

See photograph, page 173

When lady apples have their brief season, I can't resist transforming them into the autumn treat of my childhood: taffy apples, or "affy tapples," as anyone who lives in the Chicago area will call them.

you'll need

12 pointed wooden skewers, about 6 inches long

A large cookie sheet, well greased or lined with nonstick baking mats (see page 16)

12 lady apples
1¼ cups sugar
1½ tablespoons unsalted butter
5 tablespoons heavy cream, warmed
¼ cup chopped peanuts (optional)

Twist the stems of the lady apples until they pull free. Stick the skewers into the stem ends of the apples so that each apple can stand upright.

Make the caramel: Pour the sugar into the center of a deep saucepan. Carefully pour ⅓ cup water around the walls of the pan, trying not to splash any sugar onto the walls. Do not stir; gently draw your finger twice through the center of the sugar, making a cross, to moisten it. Over high heat, bring to a full boil and cook without stirring until the mixture is amber-caramel in color, 5 to 10 minutes. Immediately turn off the heat and use a wooden spoon to stir in the butter. Slowly stir in the cream (it will bubble up). Let the caramel cool slightly.

Holding them by the skewers, dip each apple almost all the way into the caramel, swirling to coat. If using, spread the chopped peanuts on a plate and roll the bottom half of each apple in the peanuts to coat lightly. Rest them on the cookie sheet with the skewers pointing up. Serve on the skewers, like lollipops.

tasting trio

Raisin–Anise Biscotti

Cannelés

Taffy Lady Apples

pineapple and melon ball brochettes

MAKES 15

Somehow, slipping these juicy summer fruits onto skewers transforms them from a fruit salad into something much more fun. I remember when my mother (and, it seemed, all the other households in the neighborhood) discovered grilling on skewers: Suddenly, a new thing called shish kabob was all the rage!

These fresh fruit skewers are refreshing on their own, dressed with mint and lime juice, and they make a great garnish for other desserts. Use any ripe melon, such as Santa Claus, canteloupe, or casaba, and any ripe berry that will hold its shape on the skewer.

you'll need

A melon baller

15 to 30 very thin skewers or decorative toothpicks, depending on length

½ pineapple, peeled
½ honeydew melon, seeded
30 large blueberries
15 fresh mint leaves
1 lime, cut into wedges

Cut the pineapple into ½-inch-thick slices. Cut the slices into ½-inch cubes and discard the hard pieces that come from the core. Set aside to drain on paper towels.

Use the melon baller to make balls from the honeydew, about the same size as the pineapple chunks. On the skewers or decorative toothpicks, thread a blueberry, a piece of pineapple, a mint leaf, a melon ball, a piece of pineapple, and finally a blueberry. Chill, covered, until ready to serve, up to 8 hours. Just before serving, squeeze lime juice over the skewers.

tasting trio

Extra-Spicy Ginger Snappers

Bite-Size Cheesecakes on Lemon–Pepper–Cornmeal Crust

Brochettes

jelly doughnut holes

MAKES 30

There seems to be something primal about a dessert with a soft, warm, oozy center. Otherwise, why would we all love jelly doughnuts (and turnovers, and flourless chocolate cakes) so much?

Fresh homemade jelly doughnuts, with their fresh yeasty dough and red juicy centers, are a world apart from even the best commercial ones (and believe me, I am a huge fan of Krispy Kremes). You must taste them at least once in your life!

you'll need

Two cookie sheets

A 2-inch biscuit or cookie cutter

A deep-frying thermometer

A pastry bag fitted with a ¼-inch plain tip (see page 15)

3 cups bread flour, plus extra for dusting
1 teaspoon salt
1 (6⁄10 ounce) cake of fresh yeast, or 1 (¼-ounce) envelope of active dry yeast
3 tablespoons granulated sugar
1 cup lukewarm milk
2 eggs
3 tablespoons unsalted butter, melted
Vegetable oil for frying
1 cup strawberry or raspberry jam
Confectioners' sugar

Combine the flour and the salt in the bowl of a mixer fitted with a dough hook.

Combine the yeast, sugar, and milk in a small bowl and let it proof (foam up) for 5 minutes. Add the proofed yeast mixture to the flour. Add the eggs and butter and mix at low speed until the dough comes together and is soft, but not sticky. If the dough does seem sticky, add more flour 1 tablespoon at a time, mixing after each addition, until a soft dough forms.

Turn the dough out onto a lightly floured work surface and knead for 1 minute, until smooth and elastic. Return the dough to the mixing bowl and cover with plastic wrap (or transfer to a clean oiled bowl and cover with plastic wrap). Let the dough rise in a warm spot (such as an oven that is not on) until doubled in bulk, about 2 hours. *(The recipe can be made up to this point and refrigerated* after the kneading *up to 1 day in advance. The dough will rise slowly in the refrigerator. Bring to room temperature before proceeding.)*

Turn on the mixer for a few seconds to punch down the dough, or punch it down in the bowl with your fist. Turn it out onto a lightly floured surface and knead a few times. Roll the dough out 1 inch thick, letting it "rest" a few times during the rolling (if you handle the dough too much, the natural gluten will tighten up and make your doughnuts tough).

Lightly flour the cookie sheets. Using the cutter, well floured, cut out rounds of dough, transferring them to the cookie sheets as you work and spacing them 2 inches apart. Reroll the scraps and cut out more disks to use up the dough. Cover the doughnut holes lightly with a kitchen towel and let them rise in a warm spot until doubled in bulk, about 20 minutes.

Meanwhile, pour 3 inches of vegetable oil into a deep, heavy pot and heat it to 350 degrees. Lay out a thick layer of paper towels or brown paper bags for draining the fried doughnuts. Spoon the jam into the pastry bag.

Working in batches of 6 or 7, transfer the risen doughnut holes to the hot oil and fry until golden and puffed, turning frequently, 5 to 7 minutes. Use a slotted spoon to transfer the hot doughnut holes to the paper to drain.

When cool enough to handle, poke the tip of the pastry bag into the center of each doughnut hole (entering from the side). Squeeze in a little jam. Serve as soon as possible.

tasting trio

Coffee Suckers on Cinnamon Sticks

Double-Vanilla Crème Brûlées

Jelly Doughnut Holes

tiny honey biscuits with crème fraîche and berries

MAKES 20 TO 25

Strawberry shortcake in a bite-size disguise. You get all the elements—flaky biscuit, pillowy cream, and juicy-ripe berries—in one mouthful, plus a golden drizzle of honey. This easy recipe makes marvelously light biscuits, lifted with whipped cream and barely flavored with honey and lemon zest. Let the biscuits turn a pale gold in the oven; the color will be gorgeous with the berries and crème fraîche. Crème fraîche, a more tangy, dense French sour cream, has become common in supermarket dairy cases, but sour cream or whipped cream can be substituted. I like to mix red and blue berries together such as blueberries, blackberries, huckleberries, raspberries, and strawberries.

you'll need

A small round cookie or biscuit cutter, 1 to 1½ inches in diameter

A large cookie sheet, well greased or lined with parchment paper or with nonstick baking mats (see page 16); or a nonstick cookie sheet

FOR THE BISCUITS

1½ cups all-purpose flour
½ teaspoon salt
4 teaspoons baking powder
¼ teaspoon freshly grated lemon zest
1 cup chilled heavy cream
2 tablespoons honey

FOR THE TOPPING

1 cup crème fraîche
1½ cups ripe raspberries, blueberries, or cut-up strawberries, or ½ cup of each kind of berry
2 tablespoons honey

Heat the oven to 400 degrees.

Make the biscuits: Mix the flour, salt, baking powder, and lemon zest together in a large bowl. Whip the cream with the honey until stiff and gently mix into the dry ingredients just until the mixture is moistened and comes together. Turn out onto a lightly floured work surface and knead a few times to bring the dough together into a ball.

Reflour the work surface and flour a rolling pin. Roll the dough out 1 inch thick. Use the cutter to cut out biscuits and transfer them to the cookie sheet. Reroll the scraps and continue cutting until all the dough is used. Bake until the biscuits are golden brown, about 15 minutes. Let them cool on a wire rack.

When ready to serve, split the biscuits in half horizontally. Place the bottoms on serving plates. On each, place a spoonful of crème fraîche and top with one raspberry, one blueberry, and one piece of strawberry. Drizzle with honey. Place the top halves of the biscuits on top. Serve immediately.

tasting trio

Chocolate Soufflé Pots

Coffee Suckers on Cinnamon Sticks

Tiny Honey Biscuits with Crème Fraîche

cranberry and cream jelly hearts

MAKES 30 TO 40

If you've never thought of Jell-O as an elegant dessert option, present these jewels at a Valentine's Day dinner or engagement party. The hearts glow ruby red on a white plate and the taste is bright and fresh. A swirl of rich cream balances out the sweet cranberry tang.

you'll need

- A shallow dish, 8 x 8 inches or a little bigger, buttered and lined with plastic wrap
- A small heart-shaped cookie cutter

2½ cups cranberry juice
2 tablespoons powdered gelatin
½ cup crème fraîche
2 teaspoons sugar
1 tablespoon raspberry purée, for garnish (optional)

Pour the cranberry juice into a saucepan (or a microwaveable bowl) and sprinkle the gelatin over the top. Set aside for 5 minutes, then heat until the gelatin is dissolved, about 1 minute. (Or, heat the mixture in a bowl in the microwave for about 30 seconds.)

Strain the mixture into the lined dish. The mixture should be about ¼ inch thick. Chill until set, about 1 to 2 hours.

Meanwhile, stir the crème fraîche and sugar together and chill.

When ready to serve, use the cookie cutter to cut out small hearts from the cranberry gelatin. Lift them out with a spatula. Arrange 2 or 3 hearts on each serving plate. Next to the hearts, put a dollop of sweetened crème fraîche. Put a large drop of raspberry purée in the center of the dollop. Drag a toothpick through it to make a heart shape.

fannie's banana–blueberry–sour cream salad

MAKES 4 TO 6 SERVINGS

Sour cream seems to be a specialty of Jewish grandmothers: Gale's Grandma Elsie and Julia's Grandma Fannie are both addicted to its creamy tang and use it often in desserts. Grandma Fannie used to serve this simple, filling fruit salad as lunch on hot days.

You can find fresh or frozen banana leaves easily in Latin and Asian markets.

2 bananas
2 cups (1 pint) blueberries, picked over for stems
½ cup sour cream
2 tablespoons orange juice
2 tablespoons maple syrup
½ teaspoon lemon juice
1 fresh or frozen banana leaf (optional)
Lemon or orange wedges, for garnish (optional)

you'll need

4 to 6 wide, short (low-ball) glasses

Cut the bananas into bite-size wedges (each wedge shaped like a section of orange): Instead of slicing straight down, slice at an angle and reverse the angle with each cut. Place the wedges in a bowl. Add the blueberries. Stir together the sour cream, orange juice, maple syrup, and lemon juice in a small bowl. Fold the mixture into the fruit. Chill.

To make banana-leaf cones, cut the leaf into 7-inch squares. Wrap two adjacent corners together to make the leaf into a cone and place in a low-ball glass to hold the shape. When ready to serve, fill the cones with salad. If using, place a wedge of lemon or orange (or one of each) on the edge of the glass.

tasting trio

Raspberry Smallovers

Orange–Honey-Glazed Almonds

Fannie's Salad

petit popovers with peach butter

MAKES ABOUT 30

See photograph, page 174

Preserving your own jam can be a daunting prospect, but fruit butters are a breeze to make—and a great way to preserve the sweet summer harvest. Cook the ripest fruit (I love peaches and apricots for this) with sugar until thick, then blend well with fluffy butter and freeze—no messing around with jars and boiling water. The frozen fruit butter, its bright flavor intact, will last you right through the fall and winter.

This eggy batter produces a tender, crusty popover that rises well above the rim of your mini-muffin cups. Each buttered popover makes a warm, sweet, rich mouthful. I like these best for breakfast and afternoon tea, but they are also a comforting dessert in cool weather, especially after a hearty soup dinner.

you'll need

2 mini-muffin tins, preferably nonstick, thickly buttered

FOR THE PEACH BUTTER

1 large peach, peeled, pitted, and diced
1 tablespoon orange juice
1 tablespoon sugar
8 ounces (2 sticks) unsalted butter, cut into pieces
½ cup confectioners' sugar

FOR THE POPOVERS

2 eggs
1 cup milk
1 cup all-purpose flour
¼ teaspoon salt
1 tablespoon sugar
2 tablespoons unsalted butter, melted

Confectioners' sugar, for dusting (optional)

Make the peach butter: Combine the peach, orange juice, and granulated sugar in a small, heavy saucepan and bring to a boil. Turn down the heat and simmer until the peach is tender and cooked down to a jam-like consistency, 20 to 25 minutes. Let the mixture cool to room temperature.

Cream the butter in a food processor or mixer until light and fluffy. Add the peach mixture and blend well to make a "compound" butter. Add the confectioners' sugar and process to blend. Chill in a serving pot or individual ramekins until ready to use. Remove from the refrigerator 30 minutes before serving.

Make the popovers: Heat the oven to 450 degrees. Whisk the eggs and milk together in a medium bowl. Add the flour, salt, and sugar and whisk to blend. Whisk in the melted butter.

Fill the buttered mini-muffin cups almost to the top with batter. Bake for 10 minutes, then reduce the heat to 350 degrees and bake until puffed and golden brown, 5 to 10 minutes more. Serve the popovers hot, with peach butter. Dust with confectioners' sugar, if desired.

tasting trio

Red, White, and Blueberry Salad

Myrna's Toasted Coconut–Chocolate Bars

Petit Popovers with Peach Butter

apricot tartes tatin

MAKES 12

The combination of ripe fruit, amber caramel, and flaky puff pastry makes *tarte Tatin* one of the world's perfect desserts. Apples are traditional, but I love the tang and texture of a good apricot even more, especially in the summer. Apricot tarte Tatin is a bit simpler than the original, since there's no need to cook apricots beforehand. Peaches and nectarines can be used as well.

Pour an easy cinnamon–vanilla caramel into individual baking dishes, then bake it with ripe apricot halves. The store-bought puff pastry tops go on for just the very end of the baking. This dessert is even better if you make it in advance: Baking brings out the pectin in the fruit, which thickens the caramel as it cools into a rich, flavorful sauce. A gentle rewarming brings the dessert back to peak perfection.

8 tablespoons (1 stick) unsalted butter
1 cup sugar
½ vanilla bean, split lengthwise
1 cinnamon stick, 2 to 3 inches
1 tablespoon vanilla brandy or plain brandy
1 tablespoon lemon juice
¼ teaspoon freshly grated orange zest
18 apricots, halved and pitted
2 sheets of puff pastry

you'll need

- 12 ramekins (see page 19)
- A cookie sheet

Melt the butter in a saucepan until it bubbles. Add the sugar and stir with a wooden spoon until smooth. Add the vanilla bean and cinnamon stick and stir to combine, pressing on the vanilla bean to bring out the seeds (I call it vanilla "caviar") inside. Continue simmering until the mixture is caramel in color, about 5 minutes. The mixture might not look smooth and blended at this point.

Stir in the brandy and lemon juice and continue cooking until smooth, about 5 minutes more.

Heat the oven to 375 degrees and arrange the ramekins on the cookie sheet. Pour 2 tablespoons of caramel into the bottom of each ramekin. Arrange three apricot halves in each ramekin. Pour a little more caramel over the apricots and bake until the caramel is bubbling and the apricots are almost tender, 15 to 20 minutes. *(The recipe can be made up to this point, cooled to room temperature, and refrigerated overnight. Bring to room temperature before proceeding.)*

Meanwhile, use a sharp knife or cutter to cut the puff pastry into 12 rounds, slightly larger than the diameter of the ramekins (the pastry will shrink during the baking).

Remove the ramekins from the oven and turn the oven up to 425 degrees. Top each ramekin with a round of puff pastry and bake until the pastry is golden brown, about 10 minutes more. Let the tarts cool for at least 1 hour or up to 8 hours.

When ready to serve, rewarm the tarts slightly to loosen the caramel: Place them in a shallow pan of very hot water, or on a flame tamer on your stovetop, set over medium heat. Unmold upside down onto small plates and serve, with the apricots up and the pastry on the bottom. The caramel will drip down a bit to form a sauce on the plate.

tasting trio

Black-and-White Chocolate Mousse Cups

Vanilla-Crusted Strawberries

Apricot Tartes Tatin

little apple brown betties

MAKES 8 TO 10 SMALL SERVINGS

Apple Brown Betty sounds—if such a thing is possible—even more American than apple pie. But the brown bread in the recipe is the giveaway: It's really as British as plum pudding.

you'll need

8 to 10 ramekins (see page 19)

A cookie sheet

- 1½ pounds tart, firm apples such as McIntosh or Granny Smith
- 4 slices whole wheat bread
- 8 tablespoons (1 stick) cold unsalted butter, slightly softened at room temperature
- ½ cup (packed) light brown sugar
- Ice cream for serving (optional)

Heat the oven to 375 degrees.

Peel, core, and slice the apples into ¼-inch slices. Place the bread slices in a food processor and pulse into fine crumbs, or chop fine with a sharp knife.

Using about 2 tablespoons of the butter, generously butter the ramekins, then sprinkle the bottoms and sides liberally with brown sugar. Make a layer of sliced apples, sugar, and finally the bread crumbs. Thickly sprinkle the tops with sugar and dot with the remaining butter. Sprinkle about 1 teaspoon water over each top.

Arrange the dishes on the cookie sheet and bake until well browned, 45 minutes to 1 hour. Serve warm, with ice cream if desired.

tasting trio

Nutmeg Ice Cream with Gingerbread Wafers

Maytag Blue Grapes

Little Apple Brown Betties

clementines in mint syrup

MAKES 6 TO 8 SERVINGS

Every parent knows that a kid who is given the choice between a fresh, wholesome orange and a syrupy can of mandarin segments will go for the can every time. I always did: Those juicy little jewels seemed infinitely more exciting than a plain old orange. This refreshing fruit salad is somewhere in between the two. Make your own syrup (with mint, if you like, but you can leave it plain), then pour it over tiny clementine sections. Served cold, it's a burst of juicy citrus, great with ice creams and cookies.

6 clementines, peeled and sectioned, white strings removed
1½ cups sugar
½ cup honey
1 tablespoon fresh mint leaves or 2 mint teabags
Fresh mint sprigs, for garnish

Put the clementine sections in a heat-proof bowl.

Combine 4 cups water with the sugar, honey, and mint in a saucepan and bring to a boil. Immediately pour the mixture through a strainer into the bowl that holds the clementine sections. Let the mixture cool to room temperature and chill, covered, until ready to serve. *(The recipe can be made up to this point up to 1 day in advance.)*

Transfer to a serving dish and garnish with mint sprigs. Serve cold.

tasting trio

Devil's Peaks with Double-Chocolate Drizzle

Chewy Butter Caramels

Clementines in Mint Syrup

sugar-frosted frozen grapes

MAKES 40

A martini glass full of these grapes, with their pale green color and sparkly frost of sugar, is a perfectly refreshing dessert after a rich meal. Pop one in your mouth and savor the juicy, cold–sweet explosion.

40 large, unblemished green grapes
⅓ cup egg whites (from about 2 eggs)
5 drops (scant ⅛ teaspoon) fresh lemon juice
2 cups granulated sugar

At least 3 hours and up to 7 days before serving, remove the grapes from their stems and place them in the freezer.

When ready to serve, whisk the egg whites with the lemon juice in a large bowl until frothy. Put the sugar in another bowl.

Drop the grapes into the bowl of egg whites, then pour the contents of the bowl through a strainer to drain the liquid. Dump the grapes onto a paper towel and roll them around until most of the excess egg white has been absorbed.

Working in batches, add the grapes to the sugar and shake them around to coat. Shake off any excess.

Transfer to serving glasses and serve immediately.

tasting trio

Pecan-Crusted Goat Cheese with Quince Compote

Raisin–Anise Biscotti

Sugar-Frosted Frozen Grapes

vanilla-crusted strawberries

MAKES ABOUT 30

Since the strawberries we can buy are usually not quite as ripe as they should be, I like to bring up their flavor with a sprinkle of sugar and smooth out any extra acidity with the rounded fragrance of vanilla. The fresh white shirt that the strawberries wear after the sugar dipping is a pretty perk.

Vanilla sugar—simply superfine sugar infused with a vanilla bean—is a standard ingredient in European pantries; it's used plain on fruit but also in baking, hot chocolate, and many other recipes where we Americans would use vanilla extract.

you'll need
A cookie sheet

1 vanilla bean, split lengthwise
2 cups superfine sugar
⅓ cup egg whites (from about 2 eggs)
5 drops (scant ⅛ teaspoon) lemon juice
About 30 ripe, firm strawberries with nice green tops

At least a day or up to a month in advance, make the vanilla sugar: Put the vanilla bean in a jar and pour the superfine sugar over it. Cover tightly and let sit at room temperature overnight or for up to a month.

When ready to make the strawberries, remove the vanilla bean and place the vanilla sugar in a bowl. (The vanilla bean can be used again.) Whisk the egg whites with the lemon juice in another bowl until frothy. Holding the berries by their green tops, dip them in the egg whites one at a time, just up to their shoulders. Let the excess egg white drip off. Roll in the vanilla sugar to coat evenly and transfer to the cookie sheet, resting the berries point side up. Let the berries sit at room temperature until dry to the touch, and serve the same day.

tasting trio

Bread Puddings with Orange Marmalade

Biscotti Milano

Vanilla-Crusted Strawberries

vacherins with raspberries and cream

MAKES ABOUT 80

See photograph, page 172

This dessert is all about putting the perfect raspberry—my favorite fruit—on a pedestal. The pedestal is a tiny mound of crisp white meringue and pillowy whipped cream, which allows the berry to glow red and dewy on top. Each mouthful is soft, crisp, juicy, and creamy.

Vacherins, an easy French classic, are like a much lighter and more elegant berry shortcake. The little white-and-red cups look beautiful on a serving plate. Crown each one with a tiny mint leaf, if you like.

You'll need to start this recipe a day ahead.

you'll need

- A pastry bag fitted with a small (¼-inch or less) plain tip
- A large cookie sheet lined with parchment paper or with nonstick baking mats (see page 16); or a nonstick cookie sheet

½ cup egg whites (from about 4 eggs), at room temperature
½ cup granulated sugar
⅓ cup confectioners' sugar, sifted
1 cup chilled heavy cream
1 pint raspberries
Tiny mint sprigs or leaves, for garnish (optional)

At least a day and up to 5 days before you plan to serve the dessert, heat the oven to 300 degrees for at least 15 minutes, then turn it off and leave the door closed. Mix the egg whites until foamy in a mixer fitted with a whisk attachment. Add the granulated sugar and whip until stiff and glossy, about 3 minutes. Add the confectioners' sugar and whip very briefly—5 to 10 seconds, just to incorporate.

Spoon the mixture into the pastry bag and pipe a small round or base of meringue, ½ inch in diameter, onto the cookie sheet. Then pipe a ring of meringue around the edge of the base and spiral upward and around one more time, making a tiny cup that is two rows high. Continue making these little cups in rows on the cookie sheet. Transfer the sheet to the turned-off oven, close the door, and leave overnight to dry until crisp. *(The recipe can be made up to this point and stored at room temperature in an airtight container for up to 5 days.)*

When ready to serve, whip the cream and pipe or spoon it into the cups. Top each cup with a raspberry. Tuck a mint leaf into each one.

tasting trio

Chocolate Pots-de-Crème

Profiteroles with Caramel Caps

Vacherins with Raspberries and Cream

Bite-Size Cheesecakes on Lemon–Pepper–Cornmeal Crusts

Strawberry Cheesecake Croquettes

Blue Cheese Fritters with Pear Salad ◎ Maytag Blue Grapes

Sweet Ricotta Fritters

Reblochon Toasts with Cinnamon–Champagne Apricots

Pecan-Crusted Goat Cheese with Quince Compote

Tomme de Savoie on Crispy Oat Rounds

Gougères with Plum Jam

The Best Cheese Crackers with Walnut-Stuffed Figs

cheese BITES

bite-size cheesecakes on lemon-pepper–cornmeal crusts

MAKES 24 TO 30

Pastry chefs are always trying to come up with a foolproof way to make cheesecake with bottom crust that's crisp—and that stays that way.

My cheesecakes combine a round of pastry with a disk of cheese filling at the very last moment. The separate elements can be completed three or four days in advance. I love this combination, with its faintly peppery, crumbly crust, mild milky cheese, and an intense hit of candied lemon on top.

you'll need

A biscuit or cookie cutter, slightly larger in diameter than the mini-muffin cups

A large cookie sheet, ungreased

2 mini-muffin tins

FOR THE CRUST

6 tablespoons cool unsalted butter, cut into pieces
¼ cup sugar
1 egg
½ teaspoon pure vanilla extract
1 cup plus 2 tablespoons all-purpose flour
1¼ cups polenta, or yellow cornmeal if unavailable
Freshly grated zest of ½ lemon
½ teaspoon freshly ground black pepper
Pinch of salt

FOR THE FILLING

1 pound cream cheese, at room temperature
½ cup sugar
2 eggs
⅛ teaspoon pure vanilla extract
1 tablespoon all-purpose flour
Pinch of salt
½ recipe lemon confit (see page 83), finely chopped, for garnish (optional)

Make the crust: Cream the butter until soft and smooth in a mixer fitted with a paddle attachment. Add the sugar and continue creaming until light and fluffy. Mix in the egg and the vanilla. In a separate bowl, stir together the dry ingredients. Add the dry ingredients to the mixer and mix at low speed until almost blended. Turn the dough out onto a work surface and knead briefly, just until the dough comes together. Form into a disk, wrap in plastic wrap, and chill for at least 2 hours or overnight.

Flour a work surface. Roll out the dough ⅛ inch thick and prick all over with a fork. Use a cutter to cut out rounds of pastry that are the same diameter as the mini-muffin cups. Transfer the pastry rounds to the cookie sheet and chill for 30 minutes.

Heat the oven to 375 degrees. Bake the pastry rounds until light golden brown, about 20 minutes. Let them cool. Leave the oven on.

Butter the mini-muffin tins and then lay a large piece of plastic wrap over the tin. Push the plastic wrap down into each cup (this is to line it very well). Don't worry—the plastic wrap will not burn or melt in the oven.

Make the filling: Whip the cream cheese until light and fluffy in a mixer fitted with a whisk attachment. Add the sugar and mix. Mix in the eggs and vanilla, then the flour and salt. Divide the filling among the lined cups, filling each one to the top. Bake for 20 minutes. Let the filling cool to room temperature, then chill.

When ready to serve, cut the plastic wrap so you can remove each cup of cheesecake individually. Lift each one out of the cup and invert onto a cornmeal crust. Peel off the plastic wrap. When all the cakes have been assembled, top each one with a tiny mound of lemon confit and serve.

tasting trio

Ruby Raspberry Jellies

Peachy Upside-Down Cakes

Bite-Size Cheesecakes

strawberry cheesecake croquettes

MAKES 24

The crisp, brown croquette that I enjoy at diners, crunchy on the outside and tender on the inside, was a good idea that seems to have disappeared from the culinary scene. I didn't set out to reinvent the croquette, but as soon as I popped these frozen cheesecake bites out of the molds and rolled them in crumbs, they started to look delightfully familiar.

These dessert croquettes get their crunch from a cookie-and-walnut crumb coating. The filling is smooth and delicate, with a juicy berry surprise in the center.

1 pound cream cheese, at room temperature
Finely grated zest and juice of 1 lemon
1 teaspoon pure vanilla extract
⅔ cup sugar
¼ cup sour cream
1 tablespoon powdered gelatin
¾ cup heavy cream, whipped
12 strawberries, green tops removed
1 cup crushed vanilla wafers or graham cracker crumbs
1 cup ground walnuts

you'll need

2 empty ice-cube trays

24 miniature paper cupcake liners (see page 19) for serving, or toothpicks

Beat the cream cheese, lemon zest and juice, vanilla, sugar, and sour cream together in a medium bowl until very smooth.

Sprinkle the gelatin over 2 tablespoons water in a small bowl and set aside for 5 minutes. Warm in the microwave for 30 seconds (or in a saucepan over medium heat) and stir to dissolve the gelatin. Quickly mix into the cream cheese mixture. Fold the whipped cream into the cream cheese mixture.

Pour ½ inch of this filling into each of 24 ice-cube compartments. Freeze for 15 minutes to firm up. Meanwhile, cut the strawberries in half. Place a strawberry half in each compartment. Pour the remaining filling over the berries to cover and fill each compartment to the top. Freeze for at least 3 to 4 hours. *(The recipe can be made up to this point, wrapped, and kept frozen for up to 3 days.)*

Stir together the crushed wafers and walnuts on a plate. When ready to serve, pop out the croquettes and roll in the crumb coating. Place in frilled paper cups or stick each one with a toothpick, and serve.

tasting trio

Devil's Peaks with Double-Chocolate Drizzle

Chewy Butter Caramels

Strawberry Cheesecake Croquettes

blue cheese fritters with pear salad

MAKES 4 SERVINGS

See photograph, page 175

Once you acquire a taste for the earthy, salty tang of blue cheese, you can't get enough of the wonderful stuff. And if there's anything better than plain blue cheese, it's a nugget of blue cheese enrobed in a hot, crisp coating, with the cheese just starting to melt next to the crust. To recover from the intensity of the fritter, I offer a delicate, cool salad of sliced pears with herbaceous tarragon, in a light lemony syrup.

Panko, bread crumbs from Japan, really are superior for creating a shattering, light crust for fritters. Regular breadcrumbs can be substituted, but the crust will be more dense. Dipping the cheese balls three times ensures that the coating will be firm enough for successful frying.

you'll need

A deep-frying thermometer

FOR THE FRITTERS

8 ounces firm blue cheese, such as Roquefort, Maytag, or Danish Blue, chilled
2 eggs
½ cup milk
2 cups panko (Japanese bread crumbs), available at Asian markets (see Sources, page 300)
Vegetable oil, for frying

FOR THE SALAD

2 Forelle or other thin-skinned pears, cored and cut into ½-inch slices
2 tablespoons fresh lemon juice
1 teaspoon chopped fresh tarragon
1 teaspoon sugar
Pinch of salt
Pinch of freshly ground black pepper

Make the fritters: Cut the cheese into 1-inch cubes and roll each lightly between your hands to round off the corners. Chill for at least 2 hours.

Make the salad: Toss the diced pears with the remaining salad ingredients. Taste and adjust the seasonings with lemon juice, sugar, and salt. Chill until ready to serve.

Whisk the eggs in a bowl, then whisk in the milk. Place the panko in a separate bowl. Dip each cube of cheese in the egg, then toss in the bread crumbs to coat. Repeat the process to create a second and third coating. Set aside while the oil is heating. *(The recipe can be made up to this point and cooked immediately, or kept refrigerated for up to 4 hours.)*

When ready to serve, heat the oil in a deep-fryer or 2 inches of oil in a deep pot fitted with a deep-frying thermometer to 365 degrees. Working in batches of 2 or 3, drop the breaded cheese cubes into the hot oil and, moving them around often, fry them until they are evenly browned, 5 to 10 seconds. Drain on paper towels. Serve as soon as possible, with pear salad on the side.

maytag blue grapes

MAKES 20

Whether made from cow, sheep, or goat milk, blue cheeses are found in every cheese-making culture from Italy to Denmark—and even Iowa! Maytag blue cheese has been made since 1941 in Newton, Iowa, by the same enterprising family that started making Maytag appliances. The company is very serious about cheesemaking; they even import the special mold spores that make the cheese blue, *Penicillium roqueforti,* from Roquefort in France.

Maytag is a wonderful creamy, peppery cheese, but any good blue can be substituted here. This recipe is my reworking of a classic cocktail bite of whole grapes covered with blue cheese and then rolled in cracked nuts; I prefer a fruitier, smaller bite.

2 ounces Maytag blue cheese
20 large seedless grapes, green, white, or red
20 small walnut pieces
Freshly ground black pepper

Use your hands to roll the cheese into marble-size balls.

Use a very sharp knife to cut a thin slice off the bottom of each grape to give it a flat bottom to stand on. Cut off the top third of each grape and reserve. Use the tip of a knife or small spoon to make a little hollow in each grape (to hold the cheese ball). Press a ball of cheese into each hollow and dot with a piece of walnut. Sprinkle with pepper.

If you like, place the grape tops back on the grapes. Serve immediately or chill for up to 12 hours. The grapes can be served chilled or at room temperature, but do not leave out for more than 4 hours.

tasting trio

Stellar Apple Spice Cakes

Dried-Plum–Pecan Chews

Maytag Blue Grapes

sweet ricotta fritters

MAKES ABOUT 18

I first tasted sheep's-milk ricotta cheese at the Old Chatham Sheepherding Company, a delightful dairy farm in upstate New York where the milk comes from sheep (instead of cows) and the shepherds are llamas (instead of dogs). Llamas are incredibly protective by nature, and they come galloping over as soon as you get anywhere near the flock.

1 egg white
1 cup sheep's-milk or other ricotta cheese (see Sources, page 300), or fresh goat cheese
½ cup plus 2 tablespoons bread flour
6 tablespoons granulated sugar
Pinch of salt
¾ teaspoon baking powder
¼ vanilla bean, split lengthwise, insides scraped out with the tip of a sharp knife, pod reserved for another use
Vegetable oil, for frying
Confectioners' sugar, for dusting

Combine all the ingredients except the oil and confectioners' sugar in a mixer fitted with a paddle attachment and mix until smooth. Form into 1-inch balls and set aside on a cookie sheet.

Heat 2 to 3 inches of oil in a deep, heavy pot fitted with a deep-frying thermometer to 365 degrees. Working in batches to avoid crowding the pot, fry the balls until golden brown all over, moving them around in the oil to make sure they brown evenly. Remove the fritters from the oil and drain on paper towels. Dust with confectioners' sugar and serve warm.

tasting trio

Passionate Raspberry Gratin

Buttermilk–Key Lime Sherbet in Roasted Pineapple Sleeves

Sweet Ricotta Fritters

reblochon toasts with cinnamon–champagne apricots

MAKES
12

Reblochon, a buttery, nutty-tasting cheese from the mountainous French region of Savoie, has recently become available in this country. Like other imported raw-milk cheeses, Reblochon was cruelly forbidden to us Americans for many years. It's a ripe cheese with some earthy power to it, and just a hint of that stinky smell that tells you it tastes wonderful.

Aged Reblochon has a leathery rind and a solid, smooth texture (called the pâte in cheese lingo). A strong, spicy compote like this one of dried apricots and warm spices is a perfect complement. I would serve champagne to drink with this. (Of course, I would serve champagne with just about anything!)

- ½ cup dried apricots
- 1 cinnamon stick, 2 to 3 inches long, or ¼ teaspoon ground cinnamon
- 2 vanilla bean, split lengthwise
- 1 cup champagne
- ½ cup (packed) light brown sugar
- 8 peppercorns
- 1 small to medium baguette, thinly sliced on the diagonal (about 12 slices total)
- 4 ounces Reblochon, thinly sliced (see Sources, page 300), or Gruyère

you'll need

A cookie sheet

Using kitchen shears or a sharp knife, cut the apricots in half. Combine the apricot halves, cinnamon stick, vanilla bean, 2 cups water, the champagne, brown sugar, and peppercorns in a saucepan over medium heat and simmer for 20 minutes, until the apricots are tender and plump. Let the mixture cool to room temperature, then transfer it to a bowl and chill it until ready to serve (leave the apricots in the poaching liquid).

When almost ready to serve, heat the oven to 400 degrees. Place the baguette slices on the cookie sheet and toast for 5 minutes. Divide the Reblochon on top of the slices and return to the oven for 3 minutes more, until the cheese is melted and runny. Divide the toasts among serving plates. Leaving the whole seasonings in the bowl, place a spoonful of chilled apricots next to the toasts. Serve immediately.

tasting trio

White-Pepper Shortbread Cups

Sesame Brittle

Reblochon Toasts with Cinnamon–Champagne Apricots

pecan-crusted goat cheese with quince compote

MAKES 6 TO 8 SERVINGS

Spending weekends with my son at Judy Schad's Indiana goat farm, Capriole Farm Cheeserie, is a great joy. He loves the goats, I love the cheese, and we both love Judy, so it's perfect! Her cheeses have a rich, fresh, milky tang that is wonderful with fruit and nuts.

With pecans, spices, orange zest, and quince, this is a combination that you can enjoy all through the fall and winter. Quinces, which come into season in the fall, are too hard and astringent to eat raw. (They do have a wonderful scent, though; a few quinces in the kitchen will perfume your whole house.) Slow-cooking the quinces makes them turn a beautiful rose color.

you'll need
A cookie sheet

2 quinces
1½ teaspoons pink peppercorns
3 1-inch-wide strips of orange zest
1 cinnamon stick, 2 to 3 inches long
¼ cup champagne or another light white wine
1 cup sugar
8 ounces fresh goat cheese (for Capriole cheese, see Sources, page 300)
Freshly ground black pepper
1 cup chopped pecans, toasted (see page 12) and cooled

Make the compote: Peel and core the quinces, then cut into ⅛-inch slices. Combine the quinces, peppercorns, orange zest, cinnamon, champagne, sugar, and 2½ cups water in a saucepan. Bring to a simmer and cook over low heat until the quince is pink and tender, about 1 hour. Let the fruit cool in the liquid. *(The recipe can be made up to this point and kept refrigerated for up to 3 days.)*

Using your hands, roll the cheese into bite-size balls and place on the cookie sheet. Grind a little bit of black pepper over the balls.

When almost ready to serve, rewarm the compote, if desired. Spread the pecans out on a plate and roll each ball in them until coated. Arrange the balls on serving plates, lift the quince slices out of their liquid, and divide in mounds next to the balls.

tasting trio

Raspberry Smallovers

Blackberry Brown-Butter Financiers

Pecan-Crusted Goat Cheese with Compote

tomme de savoie on crispy oat rounds

MAKES
5 OR 6
SERVINGS

Rolled oats are generally cooked into soft porridge or chewy cookies, but they also make wonderfully nutty, crisp biscuits. I bind the oats with a light coat of butter and corn syrup, which hardens in the oven to a crackly coating. Quick-cooking oats are perfect here; the whole grains are pressed out more and softer, leaving more surface area to pick up the coating.

The result is sweet, salty, and nutty—a perfect background for dense, aged cheeses. The rounds have a strong character, perfect for cheese with some ripeness and tang; don't serve them with a fresh cheese or anything with herbs.

1 tablespoon corn syrup
6 tablespoons unsalted butter
⅓ cup sugar
1¼ teaspoons baking soda
1 tablespoon hot water
½ cup whole wheat flour
2 cups quick-cooking oats
4 ounces Tomme de Savoie, or another firm, nutty, aged cow or goat cheese such as Gruyère
1½ cups dates, or thinly sliced tart apples

you'll need

A large cookie sheet, well greased or lined with parchment paper or with nonstick baking mats (see page 16); or a nonstick cookie sheet
Heavy drinking glass

Heat the oven to 350 degrees.

Melt the corn syrup, butter, and sugar together in a saucepan. Dissolve the baking soda in the hot water and add it to the corn syrup–butter mixture. Stir as the mixture foams up, then turn off the heat.

Stir the flour and oats together in a bowl, then add the corn syrup–butter mixture and mix to combine. Roll into balls about the size of a walnut and transfer to the cookie sheet. Flatten the balls into cakes by pressing down on them with your palm, or flour the bottom of a heavy drinking glass and press it down on each ball. The flattened cakes should be not less than ¼ inch thick.

Bake until the rounds are crisp and lightly browned, 10 to 15 minutes. Let them cool for 5 minutes on the pan, then transfer them to a wire rack to cool completely.

When ready to serve, thinly slice the cheese. Divide on top of the oat cakes and serve with fruit on the side.

tasting trio

Fairground Apple Fritters

Sesame Brittle

Tomme de Savoie on Crispy Oat Rounds

gougères with plum jam

YIELDS 50 TO 75

The first dish I ever made by myself—I think it was from a Kraft booklet my mother had lying around—was, oddly enough, a cheese soufflé. I didn't know that soufflés were hard to make, and it wasn't. Cheese soufflés are simple because of the cheese, which lends body and structure. It was from that recipe that I picked up the trick of adding mustard to melted cheese: You don't taste the mustard, but the cheese tastes more cheesy.

A *gougère* is an irresistible, bite-size cheese soufflé, best served right out of the oven. Any tasty Swiss-style cheese will do here; *fol épi* is a young version. You can tell how old a Swiss cheese is by the size of the holes; they get larger as the cheese ages. When choosing a jam, use a mild fruit that tastes good with cheese, like plum or pear; berry jams and marmalades are too acidic.

you'll need

A pastry bag fitted with a large plain tip, optional (see page 15)

A large cookie sheet, buttered and floured or lined with parchment paper or with nonstick baking mats (see page 16); or a nonstick cookie sheet

1 cup milk
4 tablespoons unsalted butter
1 cup all-purpose flour
1 teaspoon salt
⅛ teaspoon freshly ground black pepper
4 eggs
1 cup grated *fol épi* (young Swiss cheese), Gruyère, or other Swiss cheese
1 teaspoon Dijon mustard
½ teaspoon dry mustard powder
¼ teaspoon cayenne pepper
Plum jam for serving, or another mild preserve such as apple or pear butter

Heat the milk and butter in a medium-large saucepan over medium-high heat. When the mixture simmers and the butter is melted, add the flour all at once and stir. It will become very thick. Add the salt and black pepper. Stir hard over medium heat for 1 to 2 minutes to dry out the mixture. Turn off the heat and stir to cool slightly.

Add the eggs one at a time, beating well to incorporate each egg before adding the next. Stir in the cheese, mustards, and cayenne pepper and mix until smooth. Transfer the mixture to a pastry bag.

Heat the oven to 425 degrees. Pipe the mixture onto the cookie sheet in rows of kisses, about 1 inch in diameter. Smooth out any bumps on the tops with a finger dipped in flour. *(The recipe can be made up to this point up to 8 hours in advance and refrigerated, or frozen for up to a week. Thaw at room temperature before baking.)*

Bake the gougères for 10 minutes, then reduce the heat to 375 degrees and continue baking until they are golden brown, 8 to 10 minutes more. Let them cool slightly, then slice open each gougère with a serrated knife. Fill with jam and serve warm.

tasting trio

White-Pepper Shortbread Cups

Nutmeg Ice Cream with Gingerbread Wafers

Gougères with Plum Jam

the best cheese crackers with walnut-stuffed figs

YIELDS
4 TO 6
SERVINGS

This recipe comes with two great perks: the wonderful smell of your house, and the secret knowledge of how easy it is to make. The delicate crackers have just four ingredients and can be put together well in advance. You'll want to bake them at the last minute, to serve them warm and to fill your house with the fabulous aroma of gently toasting cheese—a sure appetite-provoker either before or after a great meal.

These buttery mouthfuls—with sweet figs, rich walnuts, and warm cheese crackers—are perfect with wines that have some sweetness to them. My dear and eloquent friend Jimmy, who tasted these, remarked, "The experience of the whole is greater than the sum of its parts." It's a reliable, quick, deeply sophisticated, and easy dessert.

you'll need

A large cookie sheet, well greased or lined with parchment paper or with nonstick baking mats (see page 16); or a nonstick cookie sheet

8 tablespoons (1 stick) cool unsalted butter
¾ cup plus 2 tablespoons all-purpose flour
1 cup freshly grated Parmesan cheese
¼ teaspoon freshly ground black pepper
6 dried figs
2 teaspoons Cognac or brandy
12 walnut halves

Heat the oven to 375 degrees.

Cream the butter in a mixer fitted with a paddle attachment until smooth and fluffy. Add the flour, cheese, and pepper and mix at low speed until blended. Form the dough into a disk, wrap it in plastic wrap, and refrigerate for at least 2 hours. *(The recipe can be made up to this point and kept refrigerated for up to 2 days.)* Remove the dough from the refrigerator about 30 minutes before rolling out.

Cut the figs in half and place them in a bowl. Sprinkle with the Cognac and let sit at room temperature for 30 minutes. Push a walnut half into the center of each fig half until it is embedded.

On a well-floured surface, roll out the dough into a rough rectangle, a little less than ¼ inch thick. The dough is somewhat delicate and may crack in places, but you can just push the edges together with your fingers. Carefully transfer the dough to the cookie sheet and prick evenly all over with a fork. Cut with a pizza cutter or a knife into 1½-inch squares, making a grid.

Bake just until the crackers turn golden, 15 to 20 minutes. As they come out of the oven, run your pizza cutter or knife again along the grid to separate the crackers (the edges will have baked together a little bit in the oven). Let them cool on the pan, then gently separate the crackers with your hands. They will be slightly fragile.

Serve the crackers with the stuffed figs.

tasting trio

Vacherins with Raspberries and Cream

Roasted Plums on the Half Shell with Fromage Blanc

Cheese Crackers with Figs

sources

For miniature baking molds, nonstick baking mats, cookie cutters, good-quality nonstick cookie sheets, and other kitchen equipment, these are the best catalogs:

Williams-Sonoma, 800-541-2233
JB Prince, 800-473-0577
The Baker's Catalogue (King Arthur Flour Co.), 800-827-6836
Chef's Catalog, 800-338-3232

For spices, vanilla beans, and pure extracts, such as vanilla, lemon, and orange:

The Spice House
Phone: 847-328-3711
Fax: 847-328-3631
Internet: www.thespicehouse.com
Or
Kalustyan Orient Export Trading Corp.
Phone: 212-685-3451

For fresh and aged goat cheeses:

Capriole Farm and Cheeserie, Inc.
Phone: 800-448-4628

For fresh and aged sheep's-milk cheeses, including ricotta:

Old Chatham Sheepherding Company
Phone: 518-794-7733

For Reblochon cheese from France, balsamic fruit vinegars, and Japanese bread crumbs (panko):

Dean & DeLuca
Phone: 800-221-7714
Fax: 800-781-4050
Internet: www.deananddeluca.com

For balsamic fruit vinegars:

Williams-Sonoma, 800-541-2233

For colored sugars and ascorbic acid:

The Baker's Catalogue
(King Arthur Flour Co.)
Phone: 800-827-6836
Fax: 800-343-3002
Internet: www.kingarthurflour.com

index

Note: Page numbers in **boldface** refer to photographs.